Bread for the Journey

· ·

OTHER BOOKS
BY HENRI J. M. NOUWEN

Henri J. M. Nouwen

Bread for the Journey

A Daybook of Wisdom
and Faith

HarperSanFrancisco

A Division of HarperCollins*Publishers*

BREAD FOR THE JOURNEY: *A Daybook of Wisdom and Faith.* Copyright © 1997 by Henri J. M. Nouwen. All rights reserved. Printed in the United States of America. No part of this book may be used or reproduced in any manner whatsoever without written permission except in the case of brief quotations embodied in critical articles and reviews. For information address HarperCollins Publishers, 10 East 53rd Street, New York, NY 10022.

HarperCollins Web Site: http://www.harpercollins.com

HarperCollins®, 📖 ®, and HarperSanFrancisco™ are trademarks of HarperCollins Publishers.

FIRST HARPERCOLLINS PAPERBACK EDITION PUBLISHED IN 2006

Library of Congress Cataloging-in-Publication Data is available.
ISBN-13: 978–0–06–066359–9
ISBN-10: 0–06–066359–6

06 07 08 09 10 RRD(H) 10 9 8 7 6 5 4 3 2 1

Table of Contents

A Short Story About the Writing of This Book

APRIL

AUGUST

A Short Story About
the Writing of This Book

Writing this yearbook became a true spiritual adventure for me. It felt like going on a journey without knowing how long it would be, how far away it would lead me, or where I would finally end up. When my friends at Harper San Francisco asked me if they could compose a yearbook with 365 quotations from my already published books, I replied, without realizing the full implications of what I said, "I don't want you to use old texts, I will write new ones!" They laughed and responded, "Well, that might be a little ambitious. Why don't you write some new reflections, and we'll complete them with things you have already written?" But in my stubbornness I insisted, "No, no, everything should be new."

In September 1995 I wrote my first reflection. I had bought a small, beautifully bound blank book with a picture of a piece of art from the Metropolitan Museum in New York on the cover. It had 80 white, acid-free sheets, 160 pages. I disciplined myself to write one complete reflection on every right-hand page, so that each reflection could be read independently from the others and each have its beginning, middle, and end on the same page. The blank pages on the left hand I kept free for later changes and corrections.

At first it all seemed just fun! I wrote about prayer, solitude, silence, and other familiar subjects. I wrote what came to mind spontaneously without worrying about sequence, order, or overall plan. My little book, which I carried with me wherever I went, became like a companion with whom I had intimate conversations. I tried to have at least three of these conversations a day. By the end of September my blank book was full and I felt quite proud of myself. But then it dawned on me that I would have to fill nearly five of these books to have enough texts for a whole year. Three hundred and sixty-five days suddenly seemed a frighteningly long journey. Sure, I had a few more thoughts, but 285 more seemed quite a challenge. Did I have that many ideas?

I tried to overcome my anxiety by buying more museum blank books, hoping that these books would help me write! Then I just sat down each morning, whether I had any ideas or not, and waited until my pen started to move and pull words out of my mind and heart. I didn't plan to write about Jesus. I felt the book should be written in the Spirit of Jesus but not alienate those for whom the Name of Jesus was a stumbling block. I wanted to please everybody! But my pen told me differently. After having written a whole blank book about general themes, I found myself writing about Jesus, the center of my faith. And then, to my surprise, I was asking myself, How do we become connected with Jesus? Soon I found myself writing about Word and Sacrament. But where are they held? In the Church. I had never before written about the Church! It seemed an unsafe subject to talk about, but here I was breaking through my own fears and apprehensions. The questions became, Where is the Church supposed to lead us? What about death, the resurrection, the communion of saints, heaven, hell, the second coming of Christ, and the end of times? I shivered thinking about it all! But my pen said, "Don't be afraid. Your notebooks are happy to hear what you think about it all." And so I wrote, faster and faster. By the time December came, I had written 387 reflections, even though a year has only 365 or 366 days. When I started rereading them all, I realized that I had used the yearbook to express my faith and write my own creed!

After this fast outpouring of myself, a lot of slow work needed to be done, and four people helped me to do it. Kathy Christie, my secretary, spent many days putting all these words in the word processor and many more days adding hundreds of changes and corrections. Susan Brown line-edited every reflection, cut out repetitive phrases, irrelevant thoughts, and poorly written texts, and added order to spontaneity. Ginny Hall helped me title each reflection and create a table of contents, and Wendy Greer gave much of her time to add the finishing touch. Without them this yearbook would never have been completed. I am deeply grateful for their generous help.

Writing this yearbook was an adventure indeed. But it was an adventure in solitude. It asked not only for a lot of free time but also for quiet, peaceful space. Hans and Margaret Kruitwagen, Robert Jonas and Margaret Bullitt-Jonas, Sarah Doering, and Peggy McDonnell offered me their homes in Oakville, Ontario, Watertown, Massachusetts, and Peapack, New Jersey, to find that space. Their friendship, generosity, and willingness to leave me alone most of the time were invaluable gifts.

I hope that you who read this book will discover many connections between your journey and my own and find new encouragement to live your life with trust, with hope, and especially with an always deeper love.

Bread for the Journey

. . . .

JANUARY

....

Expecting a Surprise

Each day holds a surprise. But only if we expect it can we see, hear, or feel it when it comes to us. Let's not be afraid to receive each day's surprise, whether it comes to us as sorrow or as joy. It will open a new place in our hearts, a place where we can welcome new friends and celebrate more fully our shared humanity.

Our Spiritual Parents

Joy and sorrow are never separated. When our hearts rejoice at a spectacular view, we may miss our friends who cannot see it, and when we are overwhelmed with grief, we may discover what true friendship is all about. Joy is hidden in sorrow and sorrow in joy. If we try to avoid sorrow at all costs, we may never taste joy, and if we are suspicious of ecstasy, agony can never reach us either. Joy and sorrow are the parents of our spiritual growth.

❧

Vulnerable, Like a Bird

Life is precious. Not because it is unchangeable, like a diamond, but because it is vulnerable, like a little bird. To love life means to love its vulnerability, asking for care, attention, guidance, and support. Life and death are connected by vulnerability. The newborn child and the dying elder both remind us of the preciousness of our lives. Let's not forget the preciousness and vulnerability of life during the times we are powerful, successful, and popular.

Fruits That Grow in Vulnerability

There is a great difference between successfulness and fruitfulness. Success comes from strength, control, and respectability. A successful person has the energy to create something, to keep control over its development, and to make it available in large quantities. Success brings many rewards and often fame. Fruits, however, come from weakness and vulnerability. And fruits are unique. A child is the fruit conceived in vulnerability, community is the fruit born through shared brokenness, and intimacy is the fruit that grows through touching one another's wounds. Let's remind one another that what brings us true joy is not successfulness but fruitfulness.

Living the Moment
to the Fullest

Patience is a hard discipline. It is not just waiting until something happens over which we have no control: the arrival of the bus, the end of the rain, the return of a friend, the resolution of a conflict. Patience is not a waiting passivity until someone else does something. Patience asks us to live the moment to the fullest, to be completely present to the moment, to taste the here and now, to be where we are. When we are impatient we try to get away from where we are. We behave as if the real thing will happen tomorrow, later and somewhere else. Let's be patient and trust that the treasure we look for is hidden in the ground on which we stand.

Spiritual Choices

Choices. Choices make the difference. Two people are in the same accident and severely wounded. They did not choose to be in the accident. It happened to them. But one of them chose to live the experience in bitterness, the other in gratitude. These choices radically influenced their lives and the lives of their families and friends. We have very little control over what happens in our lives, but we have a lot of control over how we integrate and remember what happens. It is precisely these spiritual choices that determine whether we live our lives with dignity.

The Gift of Friendship

Friendship is one of the greatest gifts a human being can receive. It is a bond beyond common goals, common interests, or common histories. It is a bond stronger than sexual union can create, deeper than a shared fate can solidify, and it can be even more intimate than the bonds of marriage or community. Friendship is being with the other in joy and sorrow, even when we cannot increase the joy or decrease the sorrow. It is a unity of souls that gives nobility and sincerity to love. Friendship makes all of life shine brightly. Blessed are those who lay down their lives for their friends.

Enough Light for the Next Step

Often we want to be able to see into the future. We say, "How will next year be for me? Where will I be five or ten years from now?" There are no answers to these questions. Mostly we have just enough light to see the next step: what we have to do in the coming hour or the following day. The art of living is to enjoy what we can see and not complain about what remains in the dark. When we are able to take the next step with the trust that we will have enough light for the step that follows, we can walk through life with joy and be surprised at how far we go. Let's rejoice in the little light we carry and not ask for the great beam that would take all shadows away.

Stepping over Our Wounds

Sometimes we have to "step over" our anger, our jealousy, or our feelings of rejection and move on. The temptation is to get stuck in our negative emotions, poking around in them as if we belong there. Then we become the "offended one," "the forgotten one," or the "discarded one." Yes, we can get attached to these negative identities and even take morbid pleasure in them. It might be good to have a look at these dark feelings and explore where they come from, but there comes a moment to step over them, leave them behind and travel on.

Growing Beyond Self-Rejection

One of the greatest dangers in the spiritual life is self-rejection. When we say, "If people really knew me, they wouldn't love me," we choose the road toward darkness. Often we are made to believe that self-deprecation is a virtue, called humility. But humility is in reality the opposite of self-deprecation. It is the grateful recognition that we are precious in God's eyes and that all we are is pure gift. To grow beyond self-rejection we must have the courage to listen to the voice calling us God's beloved sons and daughters, and the determination always to live our lives according to this truth.

Trusting the Catcher

Trust is the basis of life. Without trust, no human being can live. Trapeze artists offer a beautiful image of this. Flyers have to trust their catchers. They can do the most spectacular doubles, triples, or quadruples, but what finally makes their performances spectacular are the catchers who are there for them at the right time in the right place.

Much of our lives is flying. It is wonderful to fly in the air free as a bird, but when God isn't there to catch us, all our flying comes to nothing. Let's trust the Great Catcher.

The Spiritual Work of Gratitude

To be grateful for the good things that happen in our lives is easy, but to be grateful for all of our lives—the good as well as the bad, the moments of joy as well as the moments of sorrow, the successes as well as the failures, the rewards as well as the rejections—that requires hard spiritual work. Still, we are only truly grateful people when we can say thank you to all that has brought us to the present moment. As long as we keep dividing our lives between events and people we would like to remember and those we would rather forget, we cannot claim the fullness of our beings as a gift of God to be grateful for.

Let's not be afraid to look at everything that has brought us to where we are now and trust that we will soon see in it the guiding hand of a loving God.

The Still, Small Voice of Love

Many voices ask for our attention. There is a voice that says, "Prove that you are a good person." Another voice says, "You'd better be ashamed of yourself." There also is a voice that says, "Nobody really cares about you," and one that says, "Be sure to become successful, popular, and powerful." But underneath all these often very noisy voices is a still, small voice that says, "You are my Beloved, my favor rests on you." That's the voice we need most of all to hear. To hear that voice, however, requires special effort; it requires solitude, silence, and a strong determination to listen.

That's what prayer is. It is listening to the voice that calls us "my Beloved."

From Unceasing Thinking to Unceasing Prayer

Our minds are always active. We analyze, reflect, day-dream, or dream. There is not a moment during the day or night when we are not thinking. You might say our thinking is "unceasing." Sometimes we wish that we could stop thinking for a while; that would save us from many worries, guilt feelings, and fears. Our ability to think is our greatest gift, but it is also the source of our greatest pain. Do we have to become victims of our unceasing thoughts? No, we can convert our unceasing thinking into unceasing prayer by making our inner monologue into a continuing dialogue with our God, who is the source of all love.

Let's break out of our isolation and realize that Someone who dwells in the center of our beings wants to listen with love to all that occupies and preoccupies our minds.

Building Inner Bridges

Prayer is the bridge between our conscious and unconscious lives. Often there is a large abyss between our thoughts, words, and actions, and the many images that emerge in our daydreams and night dreams. To pray is to connect these two sides of our lives by going to the place where God dwells. Prayer is "soul work" because our souls are those sacred centers where all is one and where God is with us in the most intimate way.

Thus, we must pray without ceasing so that we can become truly whole and holy.

Living with Hope

Optimism and hope are radically different attitudes. Optimism is the expectation that things—the weather, human relationships, the economy, the political situation, and so on—will get better. Hope is the trust that God will fulfill God's promises to us in a way that leads us to true freedom. The optimist speaks about concrete changes in the future. The person of hope lives in the moment with the knowledge and trust that all of life is in good hands.

All the great spiritual leaders in history were people of hope. Abraham, Moses, Ruth, Mary, Jesus, Rumi, Gandhi, and Dorothy Day all lived with a promise in their hearts that guided them toward the future without the need to know exactly what it would look like. Let's live with hope.

Be Yourself

Often we want to be somewhere other than where we are, or even to be someone other than who we are. We tend to compare ourselves constantly with others and wonder why we are not as rich, as intelligent, as simple, as generous, or as saintly as they are. Such comparisons make us feel guilty, ashamed, or jealous. It is very important to realize that our vocation is hidden in where we are and who we are. We are unique human beings, each with a call to realize in life what nobody else can, and to realize it in the concrete context of the here and now.

We will never find our vocations by trying to figure out whether we are better or worse than others. We are good enough to do what we are called to do. Be yourself!

Finding Solitude

All human beings are alone. No other person will completely feel like we do, think like we do, act like we do. Each of us is unique, and our aloneness is the other side of our uniqueness. The question is whether we let our aloneness become loneliness or whether we allow it to lead us into solitude. Loneliness is painful; solitude is peaceful. Loneliness makes us cling to others in desperation; solitude allows us to respect others in their uniqueness and create community.

Letting our aloneness grow into solitude and not into loneliness is a lifelong struggle. It requires conscious choices about whom to be with, what to study, how to pray, and when to ask for counsel. But wise choices will help us to find the solitude where our hearts can grow in love.

Creating Space to Dance Together

When we feel lonely we keep looking for a person or persons who can take our loneliness away. Our lonely hearts cry out, "Please hold me, touch me, speak to me, pay attention to me." But soon we discover that the person we expect to take our loneliness away cannot give us what we ask for. Often that person feels oppressed by our demands and runs away, leaving us in despair. As long as we approach another person from our loneliness, no mature human relationship can develop. Clinging to one another in loneliness is suffocating and eventually becomes destructive. For love to be possible we need the courage to create space between us and to trust that this space allows us to dance together.

❦

Yearning for Perfect Love

When we act out of loneliness our actions easily become violent. The tragedy is that much violence comes from a demand for love. When loneliness drives our search for love, kissing easily leads to biting, caressing to hitting, looking tenderly to looking suspiciously, listening to overhearing, and surrender to rape. The human heart yearns for love: love without conditions, limitations, or restrictions. But no human being is capable of offering such love, and each time we demand it we set ourselves on the road to violence.

How then can we live nonviolent lives? We must start by realizing that our restless hearts, yearning for perfect love, can only find that love through communion with the One who created them.

❧

The Voice in the Garden of Solitude

Solitude is the garden for our hearts, which yearn for love. It is the place where our aloneness can bear fruit. It is the home for our restless bodies and anxious minds. Solitude, whether it is connected with a physical space or not, is essential for our spiritual lives. It is not an easy place to be, since we are so insecure and fearful that we are easily distracted by whatever promises immediate satisfaction. Solitude is not immediately satisfying, because in solitude we meet our demons, our addictions, our feelings of lust and anger, and our immense need for recognition and approval. But if we do not run away, we will meet there also the One who says, "Do not be afraid. I am with you, and I will guide you through the valley of darkness."

Let's keep returning to our solitude.

Community Supported
by Solitude

Solitude greeting solitude, that's what community is all about. Community is not the place where we are no longer alone but the place where we respect, protect, and reverently greet one another's aloneness. When we allow our aloneness to lead us into solitude, our solitude will enable us to rejoice in the solitude of others. Our solitude roots us in our own hearts. Instead of making us yearn for company that will offer us immediate satisfaction, solitude makes us claim our center and empowers us to call others to claim theirs. Our various solitudes are like strong, straight pillars that hold up the roof of our communal house. Thus, solitude always strengthens community.

Community, a Quality of the Heart

The word *community* has many connotations, some positive, some negative. Community can make us think of a safe togetherness, shared meals, common goals, and joyful celebrations. It also can call forth images of sectarian exclusivity, in-group language, self-satisfied isolation, and romantic naiveté. However, community is first of all a quality of the heart. It grows from the spiritual knowledge that we are alive not for ourselves but for one another. Community is the fruit of our capacity to make the interests of others more important than our own (see Philippians 2:4). The question, therefore, is not "How can we make community?" but "How can we develop and nurture giving hearts?"

Forgiveness, the Cement of Community Life

Community is not possible without the willingness to forgive one another "seventy-seven times" (see Matthew 18:22). Forgiveness is the cement of community life. Forgiveness holds us together through good and bad times, and it allows us to grow in mutual love.

But what is there to forgive or to ask forgiveness for? As people who have hearts that long for perfect love, we have to forgive one another for not being able to give or receive that perfect love in our everyday lives. Our many needs constantly interfere with our desire to be there for the other unconditionally. Our love is always limited by spoken or unspoken conditions. What needs to be forgiven? We need to forgive one another for not being God!

Receiving Forgiveness

There are two sides to forgiveness: giving and receiving. Although at first sight giving seems to be harder, it often appears that we are not able to offer forgiveness to others because we have not been able fully to receive it. Only as people who have accepted forgiveness can we find the inner freedom to give it. Why is receiving forgiveness so difficult? It is very hard to say, "Without your forgiveness I am still bound to what happened between us. Only you can set me free." That requires not only a confession that we have hurt somebody but also the humility to acknowledge our dependency on others. Only when we can receive forgiveness can we give it.

Forgiveness, the Way to Freedom

To forgive another person from the heart is an act of liberation. We set that person free from the negative bonds that exist between us. We say, "I no longer hold your offense against you." But there is more. We also free ourselves from the burden of being the "offended one." As long as we do not forgive those who have wounded us, we carry them with us or, worse, pull them as a heavy load. The great temptation is to cling in anger to our enemies and then define ourselves as being offended and wounded by them. Forgiveness, therefore, liberates not only the other but also ourselves. It is the way to the freedom of the children of God.

Healing Our Hearts Through Forgiveness

How can we forgive those who do not want to be forgiven? Our deepest desire is that the forgiveness we offer will be received. This mutuality between giving and receiving is what creates peace and harmony. But if our condition for giving forgiveness is that it will be received, we seldom will forgive! Forgiving the other is first and foremost an inner movement. It is an act that removes anger, bitterness, and the desire for revenge from our hearts and helps us to reclaim our human dignity. We cannot force those we want to forgive into accepting our forgiveness. They might not be able or willing to do so. They may not even know or feel that they have wounded us.

The only people we can really change are ourselves. Forgiving others is first and foremost healing our own hearts.

Forgiving in the Name of God

We are all wounded people. Who wounds us? Often those whom we love and those who love us. When we feel rejected, abandoned, abused, manipulated, or violated, it is mostly by people very close to us: our parents, our friends, our spouses, our lovers, our children, our neighbors, our teachers, our pastors. Those who love us wound us too. That's the tragedy of our lives. This is what makes forgiveness from the heart so difficult. It is precisely our hearts that are wounded. We cry out, "You, who I expected to be there for me, you have abandoned me. How can I ever forgive you for that?"

Forgiveness often seems impossible, but nothing is impossible for God. The God who lives within us will give us the grace to go beyond our wounded selves and say, "In the Name of God you are forgiven." Let's pray for that grace.

Healing Our Memories

Forgiving does not mean forgetting. When we forgive a person, the memory of the wound might stay with us for a long time, even throughout our lives. Sometimes we carry the memory in our bodies as a visible sign. But forgiveness changes the way we remember. It converts the curse into a blessing. When we forgive our parents for their divorce, our children for their lack of attention, our friends for their unfaithfulness in crisis, our doctors for their ill advice, we no longer have to experience ourselves as the victims of events we had no control over.

Forgiveness allows us to claim our own power and not let these events destroy us; it enables them to become events that deepen the wisdom of our hearts. Forgiveness indeed heals memories.

Choosing Joy

Joy is what makes life worth living, but for many joy seems hard to find. They complain that their lives are sorrowful and depressing. What then brings the joy we so much desire? Are some people just lucky, while others have run out of luck? Strange as it may sound, we can choose joy. Two people can be part of the same event, but one may choose to live it quite differently from the other. One may choose to trust that what happened, painful as it may be, holds a promise. The other may choose despair and be destroyed by it.

What makes us human is precisely this freedom of choice.

The Joy of Being Like Others

At first sight, joy seems to be connected with being differ-ent. When you receive a compliment or win an award, you experience the joy of not being the same as others. You are faster, smarter, or more beautiful, and it is that difference that brings you joy. But such joy is very temporary. True joy is hidden where we are the same as other people: frag-ile and mortal. It is the joy of belonging to the human race. It is the joy of being with others as a friend, a companion, a fellow traveler.

This is the joy of Jesus, who is Emmanuel: God-with-us.

FEBRUARY

Solidarity in Weakness

Joy is hidden in compassion. The word *compassion* literally means "to suffer with." It seems quite unlikely that suffering with another person would bring joy. Yet being with a person in pain, offering simple presence to someone in despair, sharing with a friend times of confusion and uncertainty . . . such experiences can bring us deep joy. Not happiness, not excitement, not great satisfaction, but the quiet joy of being there for someone else and living in deep solidarity with our brothers and sisters in this human family. Often this is a solidarity in weakness, in brokenness, in woundedness, but it leads us to the center of joy, which is sharing our humanity with others.

Being Merciful with Ourselves

We need silence in our lives. We even desire it. But when we enter into silence we encounter a lot of inner noises, often so disturbing that a busy and distracting life seems preferable to a time of silence. Two disturbing "noises" present themselves quickly in our silence: the noise of lust and the noise of anger. Lust reveals our many unsatisfied needs, anger, or many unresolved relationships. But lust and anger are very hard to face.

What are we to do? Jesus says, "Go and learn the meaning of the words: Mercy is what pleases me, not sacrifice" (Matthew 9:13). *Sacrifice* here means "offering up," "cutting out," "burning away," or "killing." We shouldn't do that with our lust and anger. It simply won't work. But we can be merciful toward our own noisy selves and turn these enemies into friends.

Befriending Our Inner Enemies

How do we befriend our inner enemies lust and anger? By listening to what they are saying. They say, "I have some unfulfilled needs" and "Who really loves me?" Instead of pushing our lust and anger away as unwelcome guests, we can recognize that our anxious, driven hearts need some healing. Our restlessness calls us to look for the true inner rest where lust and anger can be converted into a deeper way of loving.

There is a lot of unruly energy in lust and anger! When that energy can be directed toward loving well, we can transform not only ourselves but even those who might otherwise become the victims of our anger and lust. This takes patience, but it is possible.

❧

Becoming Kind

Kindness is a beautiful human attribute. When we say, "She is a kind person" or "He surely was kind to me," we express a very warm feeling. In our competitive and often violent world, kindness is not the most frequent response. But when we encounter it we know that we are blessed. Is it possible to grow in kindness, to become a kind person? Yes, but it requires discipline. To be kind means to treat another person as your "kin," your intimate relative. We say, "We are kin" or "He is next of kin." To be kind is to reach out to someone as being of "kindred" spirit.

Here is the great challenge: All people, whatever their color, religion, or sex, belong to humankind and are called to be kind to one another, treating one another as brothers and sisters. There is hardly a day in our lives in which we are not called to this.

God's Unconditional Love

What can we say about God's love? We can say that God's love is unconditional. God does not say, "I love you, if . . ." There are no *ifs* in God's heart. God's love for us does not depend on what we do or say, on our looks or intelligence, on our success or popularity. God's love for us existed before we were born and will exist after we have died. God's love is from eternity to eternity and is not bound to any time-related events or circumstances. Does that mean that God does not care what we do or say? No, because God's love wouldn't be real if God didn't care. To love without condition does not mean to love without concern. God desires to enter into relationship with us and wants us to love God in return.

Let's dare to enter into an intimate relationship with God without fear, trusting that we will receive love and always more love.

Returning to God's Ever-Present Love

We often confuse unconditional love with unconditional approval. God loves us without conditions but does not approve of every human behavior. God doesn't approve of betrayal, violence, hatred, suspicion, and all other expressions of evil, because they all contradict the love God wants to instill in the human heart. Evil is the absence of God's love. Evil does not belong to God.

God's unconditional love means that God continues to love us even when we say or think evil things. God continues to wait for us as a loving parent waits for the return of a lost child. It is important for us to hold on to the truth that God never gives up loving us even when God is saddened by what we do. That truth will help us to return to God's ever-present love.

Dressed in Gentleness

Once in a while we meet a gentle person. Gentleness is a virtue hard to find in a society that admires toughness and roughness. We are encouraged to get things done and to get them done fast, even when people get hurt in the process. Success, accomplishment, and productivity count. But the cost is high. There is no place for gentleness in such a milieu.

Gentle is the one who does "not break the crushed reed, or snuff the faltering wick" (Matthew 12:20). Gentle is the one who is attentive to the strengths and weaknesses of the other and enjoys being together more than accomplishing something. A gentle person treads lightly, listens carefully, looks tenderly, and touches with reverence. A gentle person knows that true growth requires nurture, not force. Let's dress ourselves with gentleness. In our tough and often unbending world our gentleness can be a vivid reminder of the presence of God among us.

Care, the Source of All Cure

Care is something other than cure. *Cure* means "change." A doctor, a lawyer, a minister, a social worker—they all want to use their professional skills to bring about changes in people's lives. They get paid for whatever kind of cure they can bring about. But cure, desirable as it may be, can easily become violent, manipulative, and even destructive if it does not grow out of care. Care is being with, crying out with, suffering with, feeling with. Care is compassion. It is claiming the truth that the other person is my brother or sister, human, mortal, vulnerable, like I am.

When care is our first concern, cure can be received as a gift. Often we are not able to cure, but we are always able to care. To care is to be human.

❧

Giving and Receiving Consolation

Consolation is a beautiful word. It means "to be" (*con-*) "with the lonely one" (*solus*). To offer consolation is one of the most important ways to care. Life is so full of pain, sadness, and loneliness that we often wonder what we can do to alleviate the immense suffering we see. We can and must offer consolation. We can and must console the mother who lost her child, the young person with AIDS, the family whose house burned down, the soldier who was wounded, the teenager who contemplates suicide, the old man who wonders why he should stay alive.

To console does not mean to take away the pain but rather to be there and say, "You are not alone, I am with you. Together we can carry the burden. Don't be afraid. I am here." That is consolation. We all need to give it as well as to receive it.

Dying Well

We will all die one day. That is one of the few things we can be sure of. But will we die well? That is less certain. Dying well means dying for others, making our lives fruitful for those we leave behind. The big question, therefore, is not "What can I still do in the years I have left to live?" but "How can I prepare myself for my death so that my life can continue to bear fruit in the generations that will follow me?"

Jesus died well because through dying he sent his Spirit of Love to his friends, who with that Holy Spirit could live better lives. Can we also send the Spirit of Love to our friends when we leave them? Or are we too worried about what *we* can still *do?* Dying can become our greatest gift if we prepare ourselves to die well.

Words That Create

Words, words, words. Our society is full of words: on billboards, on television screens, in newspapers and books. Words whispered, shouted, and sung. Words that move, dance, and change in size and color. Words that say, "Taste me, smell me, eat me, drink me, sleep with me," but most of all, "buy me." With so many words around us, we quickly say, "Well, they're just words." Thus, words have lost much of their power.

Still, the word has the power to create. When God speaks, God creates. When God says, "Let there be light" (Genesis 1:3), light is. God speaks light. For God, speaking and creating are the same. It is this creative power of the word we need to reclaim. What we say is very important. When we say, "I love you," and say it from the heart, we can give another person new life, new hope, new courage. When we say, "I hate you," we can destroy another person. Let's watch our words.

Words That Feed Us

When we talk to one another, we often talk about what happened, what we are doing, or what we plan to do. Often we say, "What's up?" and we encourage one another to share the details of our daily lives. But often we want to hear something else. We want to hear, "I've been thinking of you today," or "I missed you," or "I wish you were here," or "I really love you." It is not always easy to say these words, but such words can deepen our bonds with one another.

Telling someone "I love you" in whatever way is always delivering good news. Nobody will respond by saying, "Well, I knew that already, you don't have to say it again"! Words of love and affirmation are like bread. We need them each day, over and over. They keep us alive inside.

❧

Celebrating Being Alive

Birthdays are so important. On our birthdays we celebrate being alive. On our birthdays people can say to us, "Thank you for being!" Birthday presents are signs of our families' and friends' joy that we are part of their lives. Little children often look forward to their birthdays for months. Their birthdays are their big days, when they are the center of attention and all their friends come to celebrate.

We should never forget our birthdays or the birthdays of those who are close to us. Birthdays keep us childlike. They remind us that what is important is not what we do or accomplish, not what we have or who we know, but that we *are*, here and now. On birthdays let us be grateful for the gift of life.

Seeing the Beauty and Goodness in Front of Us

We don't have to go far to find the treasure we are seek-ing. There is beauty and goodness right where we are. And only when we can see the beauty and goodness that are close by can we recognize beauty and goodness on our travels far and wide. There are trees and flowers to enjoy, paintings and sculptures to admire; most of all there are people who smile, play, and show kindness and gentleness. They are all around us, to be recognized as free gifts to receive in gratitude.

Our temptation is to collect all the beauty and good-ness surrounding us as helpful information we can use for our projects. But then we cannot enjoy it, and we soon find that we need a vacation to restore ourselves. Let's try to see the beauty and goodness in front of us before we go elsewhere to look for it.

The Meal That Makes Us Family and Friends

We all need to eat and drink to stay alive. But having a meal is more than eating and drinking. It is celebrating the gifts of life we share. A meal together is one of the most intimate and sacred human events. Around the table we become vulnerable, filling one another's plates and cups and encouraging one another to eat and drink. Much more happens at a meal than satisfying hunger and quenching thirst. Around the table we become family, friends, community, yes, a body.

That is why it is so important to "set" the table. Flowers, candles, colorful napkins all help us to say to one another, "This is a very special time for us, let's enjoy it!"

The Intimacy of the Table

The table is one of the most intimate places in our lives. It is there that we give ourselves to one another. When we say, "Take some more, let me serve you another plate, let me pour you another glass, don't be shy, enjoy it," we say a lot more than our words express. We invite our friends to become part of our lives. We want them to be nurtured by the same food and drink that nurture us. We desire communion. That is why a refusal to eat and drink what a host offers is so offensive. It feels like a rejection of an invitation to intimacy.

Strange as it may sound, the table is the place where we want to become food for one another. Every breakfast, lunch, or dinner can become a time of growing communion with one another.

The Barometer of Our Lives

Although the table is a place for intimacy, we all know how easily it can become a place of distance, hostility, and even hatred. Precisely because the table is meant to be an intimate place, it easily becomes the place we experience the absence of intimacy. The table reveals the tensions among us. When husband and wife don't talk to each other, when a child refuses to eat, when brothers and sisters bicker, when there are tense silences, then the table becomes hell, the place we least want to be.

The table is the barometer of family and community life. Let's do everything possible to make the table the place to celebrate intimacy.

Creating Beautiful Memories

What happens during meals shapes a large part of our memories. As we grow older we forget many things, but we mostly remember the Thanksgiving or Christmas dinners in our families. We remember them with joy and gratitude or with sadness and anger. They remind us of the peace that existed in our homes or the conflicts that never seemed to get resolved. These special moments around the table stand out as vivid reminders of the quality of our lives together.

Today fast-food services and TV dinners have made common meals less and less central. But what will there be to remember when we no longer come together around the table to share a meal? Maybe we will have fewer painful memories, but will we have any joyful ones? Can we make the table a hospitable place, inviting us to kindness, gentleness, joy, and peace and creating beautiful memories?

❧

The Basis of Our Security

What is the basis of our security? When we start thinking about that question, we may give many answers: success, money, friends, property, popularity, family, connections, insurance, and so on. We may not always *think* that any of these forms the basis of our security, but our *actions* or *feelings* may tell us otherwise. When we start losing our money, our friends, or our popularity, our anxiety often reveals how deeply our sense of security is rooted in these things.

A spiritual life is a life in which our security is based not in any created things, good as they may be, but in God, who is everlasting love. We probably will never be completely free from our attachment to the temporal world, but if we want to live in that world in a truly free way, we'd better not belong to it. "You cannot be the slave both of God and of money" (Luke 16:13).

The Nonpossessive Life

To be able to enjoy fully the many good things the world has to offer, we must be detached from them. To be detached does not mean to be indifferent or uninterested. It means to be nonpossessive. Life is a gift to be grateful for and not a property to cling to.

A nonpossessive life is a free life. But such freedom is only possible when we have a deep sense of belonging. To whom then do we belong? We belong to God, and the God to whom we belong has sent us into the world to proclaim in his Name that all of creation is created in and by love and calls us to gratitude and joy. That is what the "detached" life is all about. It is a life in which we are free to offer praise and thanksgiving.

True Intimacy

Human relationships easily become possessive. Our hearts so much desire to be loved that we are inclined to cling to the person who offers us love, affection, friendship, care, or support. Once we have seen or felt a hint of love, we want more of it. That explains why lovers so often bicker with each other. Lovers' quarrels are quarrels between people who want more of each other than they are able or willing to give.

It is very hard for love not to become possessive because our hearts look for perfect love and no human being is capable of that. Only God can offer perfect love. Therefore, the art of loving includes the art of giving one another space. When we invade one another's space and do not allow the other to be his or her own free person, we cause great suffering in our relationships. But when we give another space to move and share our gifts, true intimacy becomes possible.

❧

The Balance Between Closeness and Distance

Intimacy between people requires closeness as well as distance. It is like dancing. Sometimes we are very close, touching each other or holding each other; sometimes we move away from each other and let the space between us become an area where we can freely move.

To keep the right balance between closeness and distance requires hard work, especially since the needs of the partners may be quite different at a given moment. One might desire closeness while the other wants distance. One might want to be held while the other looks for independence. A perfect balance seldom occurs, but the honest and open search for that balance can give birth to a beautiful dance, worthy to behold.

What Is Most Personal
Is Most Universal

We like to make a distinction between our private and public lives and say, "Whatever I do in my private life is nobody else's business." But anyone trying to live a spiritual life will soon discover that the most personal is the most universal, the most hidden is the most public, and the most solitary is the most communal. What we live in the most intimate places of our beings is not just for us but for all people. That is why our inner lives are lives for others. That is why our solitude is a gift to our community, and that is why our most secret thoughts affect our common life.

Jesus says, "No one lights a lamp to put it under a tub; they put it on the lamp stand where it shines for everyone in the house" (Matthew 5:14–15). The most inner light is a light for the world. Let's not have "double lives"; let us allow what we live in private to be known in public.

Bringing Our Secrets into the Light

We all have our secrets: thoughts, memories, feelings that we keep to ourselves. Often we think, "If people knew what I feel or think, they would not love me." These carefully kept secrets can do us much harm. They can make us feel guilty or ashamed and may lead us to self-rejection, depression, and even suicidal thoughts and actions.

One of the most important things we can do with our secrets is to share them in a safe place, with people we trust. When we have a good way to bring our secrets into the light and can look at them with others, we will quickly discover that we are not alone with our secrets and that our trusting friends will love us more deeply and more intimately than before. Bringing our secrets into the light creates community and inner healing. As a result of sharing secrets, not only will others love us better but we will love ourselves more fully.

Hidden Greatness

There is much emphasis on notoricty and fame in our society. Our newspapers and television keep giving us the
message: What counts is to be known, praised, and admired, whether you are a writer, an actor, a musician, or a
politician.

Still, real greatness is often hidden, humble, simple,
and unobtrusive. It is not easy to trust ourselves and our
actions without public affirmation. We must have strong
self-confidence combined with deep humility. Some of
the greatest works of art and the most important works
of peace were created by people who had no need for
the limelight. They knew that what they were doing was
their call, and they did it with great patience, perseverance, and love.

Facing Our Mortality

We all have dreams about the perfect life: a life without pain, sadness, conflict, or war. The spiritual challenge is to experience glimpses of this perfect life right in the middle of our many struggles. By embracing the reality of our mortal life, we can get in touch with the eternal life that has been sown there. The apostle Paul expresses this powerfully when he writes, "We are subjected to every kind of hardship, but never distressed; we see no way out but we never despair; we are pursued but never cut off; knocked down, but still have some life in us; always we carry with us in our body the death of Jesus so that the life of Jesus, too, may be visible in our . . . mortal flesh" (2 Corinthians 4:8–12).

Only by facing our mortality can we come in touch with the life that transcends death. Our imperfections open for us the vision of the perfect life that God in and through Jesus has promised us.

Creating Space for God

Discipline is the other side of discipleship. Discipleship without discipline is like waiting to run in the marathon without ever practicing. Discipline without discipleship is like always practicing for the marathon but never participating. It is important, however, to realize that discipline in the spiritual life is not the same as discipline in sports. Discipline in sports is the concentrated effort to master the body so that it can obey the mind better. Discipline in the spiritual life is the concentrated effort to create the space and time where God can become our master and where we can respond freely to God's guidance.

Thus, discipline is the creation of boundaries that keep time and space open for God. Solitude requires discipline, worship requires discipline, caring for others requires discipline. They all ask us to set apart a time and a place where God's gracious presence can be acknowledged and responded to.

Letting Go of Our Fear of God

We are afraid of emptiness. Spinoza speaks about our "horror vacui," our horrendous fear of vacancy. We like to occupy—fill up—every empty time and space. We want to be occupied. And if we are not occupied we easily become preoccupied; that is, we fill the empty spaces before we have even reached them. We fill them with our worries, saying, "But what if . . . "

It is very hard to allow emptiness to exist in our lives. Emptiness requires a willingness not to be in control, a willingness to let something new and unexpected happen. It requires trust, surrender, and openness to guidance. God wants to dwell in our emptiness. But as long as we are afraid of God and God's actions in our lives, it is unlikely that we will offer our emptiness to God. Let's pray that we can let go of our fear of God and embrace God as the source of all love.

Being Free to Love

Jesus came to us to help us overcome our fear of God. As long as we are afraid of God, we cannot love God. Love means intimacy, closeness, mutual vulnerability, and a deep sense of safety. But all of those are impossible as long as there is fear. Fear creates suspicion, distance, defensiveness, and insecurity.

The greatest block in the spiritual life is fear. Prayer, meditation, and education cannot come forth out of fear. God is perfect love, and as John the Evangelist writes, "Perfect love drives out fear" (1 John 4:18). Jesus' central message is that God loves us with an unconditional love and desires our love, free from all fear, in return.

MARCH

❦

. . . .

God's Powerlessness

Jesus is God-with-us, Emmanuel. The great mystery of God becoming human is God's desire to be loved by us. By becoming a vulnerable child, completely dependent on human care, God wants to take away all distance between the human and the divine.

Who can be afraid of a little child who needs to be fed, to be cared for, to be taught, to be guided? We usually talk about God as the all-powerful, almighty God on whom we depend completely. But God wanted to become the all-powerless, all-vulnerable God who completely depends on us. How can we be afraid of a God who wants to be "God-with-us" and wants us to become "Us-with-God"?

God's Covenant

God made a covenant with us. The word *covenant* means "coming together." God wants to come together with us. In many of the stories in the Hebrew Bible, we see that God appears as a God who defends us against our enemies, protects us against dangers, and guides us to freedom. God is *God-for-us*. When Jesus comes a new dimension of the covenant is revealed. In Jesus, God is born, grows to maturity, lives, suffers, and dies as we do. God is *God-with-us*. Finally, when Jesus leaves he promises the Holy Spirit. In the Holy Spirit, God reveals the full depth of the covenant. God wants to be as close to us as our breath. God wants to breathe in us, so that all we say, think, and do is completely inspired by God. God is *God-within-us*. Thus, God's covenant reveals to us how much God loves us.

❧

God's Faithfulness and Ours

When God makes a covenant with us, God says, "I will love you with an everlasting love. I will be faithful to you, even when you run away from me, reject me, or betray me." In our society we don't speak much about covenants; we speak about contracts. When we make a contract with a person, we say, "I will fulfill my part as long as you fulfill yours. When you don't live up to your promises, I no longer have to live up to mine." Contracts are often broken because the partners are unwilling or unable to be faithful to their terms.

But God didn't make a contract with us; God made a covenant with us, and God wants our relationships with one another to reflect that covenant. This is why marriage, friendship, and life in community are all ways to give visibility to God's faithfulness in our lives together.

Reflecting God's Perfect Love

God's love for us is everlasting. That means that God's love for us existed before we were born and will exist after we have died. It is an eternal love in which we are embraced. Living a spiritual life calls us to claim that eternal love for ourselves so that we can live our temporal loves—for parents, brothers, sisters, teachers, friends, spouses, and all people who become part of our lives—as reflections or refractions of God's eternal love. No fathers or mothers can love their children perfectly. No husbands or wives can love each other with unlimited love. There is no human love that is not broken somewhere.

When our broken love is the only love we can have, we are easily thrown into despair, but when we can live our broken love as a partial reflection of God's perfect, unconditional love, we can forgive one another our limitations and enjoy together the love we have to offer.

Creating a Home Together

Many human relationships are like the interlocking fingers of two hands. Our loneliness makes us cling to one another, and this mutual clinging makes us suffer immensely because it does not take our loneliness away. But the harder we try, the more desperate we become. Many of these "interlocking" relationships fall apart because they become suffocating and oppressive. Human relationships are meant to be like two hands folded together. They can move away from each other while still touching with the fingertips. They can create space between themselves, a little tent, a home, a safe place to be.

True relationships among people point to God. They are like prayers in the world. Sometimes the hands that pray are fully touching, sometimes there is distance between them. They always move to and from each other, but they never lose touch. They keep praying to the One who brought them together.

True Hospitality

Every good relationship between two or more people, whether it is friendship, marriage, or community, creates space where strangers can enter and become friends. Good relationships are hospitable. When we enter into a home and feel warmly welcomed, we will soon realize that the love among those who live in that home is what makes that welcome possible.

When there is conflict in the home, the guest is soon forced to choose sides. "Are you for him or for her?" "Do you agree with them or with us?" "Do you like him more than you do me?" These questions prevent true hospitality—that is, an opportunity for the stranger to feel safe and discover his or her own gifts. Hospitality is more than an expression of love for the guest. It is also and foremost an expression of love between the hosts.

The Great Gift of Parenthood

Children are their parents' guests. They come into the space that has been created for them, stay for a while—fifteen, twenty, or twenty-five years—and leave again to create their own space. Although parents speak about "our son" and "our daughter," their children are not their property. In many ways children are strangers. Parents have to come to know them, discover their strengths and their weaknesses, and guide them to maturity, allowing them to make their own decisions.

The greatest gift parents can give their children is their love for each other. Through that love they create an anxiety-free place for their children to grow, encouraging them to develop confidence in themselves and find the freedom to choose their own ways in life.

Toward a Nonjudgmental Life

One of the hardest spiritual tasks is to live without prejudices. Sometimes we aren't even aware how deeply rooted our prejudices are. We may think that we relate to people who are different from us in color, religion, sexual orientation, or lifestyle as equals, but in concrete circumstances our spontaneous thoughts, uncensored words, and knee-jerk reactions often reveal that our prejudices are still there.

Strangers, people different from us, stir up fear, discomfort, suspicion, and hostility. They make us lose our sense of security just by being "other." Only when we fully claim that God loves us in an unconditional way and look at "those other persons" as equally loved can we begin to discover that the great variety in humanity is an expression of the immense richness of God's heart. Then the need to prejudge people can gradually disappear.

Freedom from Judging, Freedom for Mercy

We spend an enormous amount of energy making up our minds about other people. Not a day goes by without somebody doing or saying something that evokes in us the need to form an opinion about him or her. We hear a lot, see a lot, and know a lot. The feeling that we have to sort it all out in our minds and make judgments about it can be quite oppressive.

The desert fathers said that judging others is a heavy burden, while being judged by others is a light one. Once we can let go of our need to judge others, we will experience an immense inner freedom. Once we are free from judging, we will be also free for mercy. Let's remember Jesus' words: "Do not judge, and you will not be judged" (Matthew 7:1).

Our Unique Call

So many terrible things happen every day that we start wondering whether the few things we do ourselves make any sense. When people are starving only a few thousand miles away, when wars are raging close to our borders, when countless people in our cities have no homes to live in, our own activities look futile. Such considerations, however, can paralyze and depress us.

Here the word *call* becomes important. We are not called to save the world, solve all problems, and help all people. But each of us has our own unique call, in our families, in our work, in our world. We have to keep asking God to help us see clearly what our call is and to give us the strength to live out that call with trust. Then we will discover that our faithfulness to a small task is the most healing response to the illnesses of our time.

Listening as Spiritual Hospitality

To listen is very hard, because it asks of us so much interior stability that we no longer need to prove ourselves by speeches, arguments, statements, or declarations. True listeners no longer have an inner need to make their presence known. They are free to receive, to welcome, to accept.

Listening is much more than allowing another to talk while waiting for a chance to respond. Listening is paying full attention to others and welcoming them into our very beings. The beauty of listening is that those who are listened to start feeling accepted, start taking their words more seriously and discovering their true selves. Listening is a form of spiritual hospitality by which you invite strangers to become friends, to get to know their inner selves more fully, and even to dare to be silent with you.

❖

The Spirit of Jesus Listening in Us

Listening in the spiritual life is much more than a psychological strategy to help others discover themselves. In the spiritual life the listener is not the ego, which would like to speak but is trained to restrain itself, but the Spirit of God within us. When we are baptized in the Spirit—that is, when we have received the Spirit of Jesus as the breath of God breathing within us—that Spirit creates in us a sacred space where the other can be received and listened to. The Spirit of Jesus prays in us and listens in us to all who come to us with their sufferings and pains.

When we dare to trust fully in the power of God's Spirit listening in us, we will see true healing occur.

❦

Absence That Creates Presence

It is good to visit people who are sick, dying, shut in, handicapped, or lonely. But it is also important not to feel guilty when our visits have to be short or can only happen occasionally. Often we are so apologetic about our limitations that our apologies prevent us from really being with the other when we are there. A short time fully present to a sick person is much better than a long time with many explanations of why we are too busy to come more often.

If we are able to be fully present to our friends when we are with them, our absence too will bear many fruits. Our friends will say, "He visited me" or "She visited me," and discover in our absence the lasting grace of our presence.

❦

Bringing the Spirit Through Leaving

It is often in our absence that the Spirit of God manifests itself. When Jesus left his disciples he said, "It is for your own good that I am going, because unless I go, the Paraclete [the Spirit] will not come to you. . . . However, when the Spirit of truth comes he will lead you to the complete truth" (John 16:7, 13). It was only in Jesus' absence that his friends discovered the full meaning of his presence. It was only in his absence that they completely understood his words and experienced full communion with him; and it was only in his absence that they could gather in a community of faith, hope, and love.

When we claim for ourselves that we come to our friends in the Name of Jesus—that through us Jesus becomes present to them—we can trust that our leaving will also bring them the Spirit of Jesus. Thus, not only our presence but also our absence becomes a gift to others.

An Honest Being-With

Being with a friend in great pain is not easy. It makes us uncomfortable. We do not know what to do or say, and we worry about how to respond to what we hear. Our temptation is to say things that come more out of our own fear than out of our care for the person in pain. Sometimes we say things like "Well, you're doing a lot better than yesterday," or "You will soon be your old self again," or "I'm sure you will get over this." But often we know that what we're saying is not true, and our friends know it too.

We do not have to play games with one another. We can simply say, "I am your friend, I am happy to be with you." We can say that in words or with touch or with loving silence. Sometimes it is good to say, "You don't have to talk. Just close your eyes. I am here with you, thinking of you, praying for you, loving you."

The Virtue of Flexibility

Trees look strong compared with the wild reeds in the field. But when the storm comes the trees are uprooted, whereas the wild reeds, while moved back and forth by the wind, remain rooted and stand up again after the storm has calmed down.

Flexibility is a great virtue. When we cling to our own positions and are not willing to let our hearts be moved back and forth a little by the ideas or actions of others, we may easily be broken. Being like wild reeds does not mean being wishy-washy. It means moving a little with the winds of the time while remaining solidly anchored in the ground. A humorless, intense, opinionated rigidity about current issues might cause them to break our spirits and make us bitter people. Let's be flexible while being deeply rooted.

Not Breaking
the Bruised Reeds

Some of us tend to do away with things that are slightly damaged. Instead of repairing them we say, "Well, I don't have time to fix it, I might as well throw it in the garbage can and buy a new one." Often we also treat people this way. We say, "Well, he has a problem with drinking; well, she is quite depressed; well, they have mismanaged their business . . . we'd better not take the risk of getting involved with them." When we dismiss people out of hand because of their apparent woundedness, we stunt their lives by ignoring their gifts, which are often buried in their wounds.

We all are bruised reeds, whether our bruises are visible or not. The compassionate life is the life in which we believe that strength is hidden in weakness and that true community is a fellowship of the weak.

❧

Coming Together in Poverty

There are many forms of poverty: economic poverty, physical poverty, emotional poverty, mental poverty, and spiritual poverty. As long as we relate primarily to one another's wealth, health, stability, intelligence, and strength, we cannot develop true community. Community is not a talent show in which we dazzle the world with our combined gifts. Community is the place where our poverty is acknowledged and accepted, not as something we have to learn to cope with as best as we can but as a true source of new life.

Living community in whatever form—family, parish, twelve-step program, or intentional community—challenges us to come together at the place of our poverty, believing that there we can reveal our richness.

The Infinite Value of Life

Some people live long lives, some die very young. Is a long life better than a short life? What truly counts is not the length of our lives but their quality. Jesus was in his early thirties when he was killed. Thérèse de Lisieux was in her twenties when she died. Anne Frank was a teenager when she lost her life. But their short lives continue to bear fruit long after their deaths.

A long life is a blessing when it is well lived and leads to gratitude, wisdom, and sanctity. But some people can live truly full lives even when their years are few. As we see so many young people die of cancer and AIDS, let us do everything possible to show our friends that, though their lives may be short, they are of infinite value.

A Still Place in the Market

"Be still and acknowledge that I am God" (Psalm 46:10). These are words to take with us in our busy lives. We may think about stillness in contrast to our noisy world. But perhaps we can go further and keep an inner stillness even while we carry on business, teach, work in construction, make music, or organize meetings.

It is important to keep a still place in the "marketplace." This still place is where God can dwell and speak to us. It also is the place from which we can speak in a healing way to all the people we meet in our busy days. Without that still space we start spinning. We become driven people, running all over the place without much direction. But with that stillness God can be our gentle guide in everything we think, say, or do.

Claiming the Sacredness
of Our Being

Are we friends with ourselves? Do we love who we are? These are important questions because we cannot develop good friendships with others unless we have befriended ourselves.

How then do we befriend ourselves? We have to start by acknowledging the truth of ourselves. We are beautiful but also limited, rich but also poor, generous but also worried about our security. Yet beyond all that we are people with souls, sparks of the divine. To acknowledge the truth of ourselves is to claim the sacredness of our being, without fully understanding it. Our deepest being escapes our own mental or emotional grasp. But when we trust that our souls are embraced by a loving God, we can befriend ourselves and reach out to others in loving relationships.

The Ways to Self-Knowledge

"Know yourself" is good advice. But to know ourselves doesn't mean to analyze ourselves. Sometimes we want to know ourselves as if we were machines that could be taken apart and put back together at will. At certain critical times in our lives it might be helpful to explore in some detail the events that led us to our crises, but we make a mistake when we think that we can ever completely understand ourselves and explain the full meaning of our lives to others.

Solitude, silence, and prayer are often the best ways to self-knowledge. Not because they offer solutions for the complexity of our lives but because they bring us in touch with our sacred center, where God dwells. That sacred center may not be analyzed. It is the place of adoration, thanksgiving, and praise.

Sharing Our Solitude

A friend is more than a therapist or a confessor, even though a friend can sometimes heal us and offer us God's forgiveness.

A friend is that other person with whom we can share our solitude, our silence, and our prayer. A friend is that other person with whom we can look at a tree and say, "Isn't that beautiful," or sit on the beach and silently watch the sun disappear under the horizon. With a friend we don't have to say or do something special. With a friend we can be still and know that God is there with both of us.

Friendship in the Twilight Zones of Our Hearts

There is a twilight zone in our own hearts that we ourselves cannot see. Even when we know quite a lot about ourselves—our gifts and weaknesses, our ambitions and aspirations, our motives and drives—large parts of ourselves remain in the shadow of consciousness.

This is a very good thing. We will always remain partially hidden to ourselves. Other people, especially those who love us, can often see our twilight zones better than we ourselves can. The way we are seen and understood by others is different from the way we see and understand ourselves. We will never fully know the significance of our presence in the lives of our friends. That's a grace, a grace that calls us not only to humility but also to a deep trust in those who love us. It is in the twilight zones of our hearts where true friendships are born.

The Healing Touch

Touch, yes, touch, speaks the wordless words of love. We receive so much touch when we are babies and so little when we are adults. Still, in friendship, touch often gives more life than words. A friend's hand stroking our back, a friend's arms resting on our shoulder, a friend's fingers wiping our tears away, a friend's lips kissing our forehead—these bring true consolation. These moments of touch are truly sacred. They restore, they reconcile, they reassure, they forgive, they heal.

Everyone who touched Jesus and everyone whom Jesus touched were healed. God's love and power went out from him (see Luke 6:19). When a friend touches us with free, nonpossessive love, it is God's incarnate love that touches us and God's power that heals us.

Becoming Friends of Our Children

Can fathers and mothers become friends of their children? Many children leave their parents to find freedom and independence and return to them only occasionally. When they return they often feel like children again and, therefore, do not want to stay long. Many parents worry about their children's well-being after they have left home. When their children visit they want to be caring parents again.

But a mother can also become the daughter of her daughter and a father the son of his son. A mother can become the daughter of her son and a father the son of his daughter. Father and mother become brother and sister of their own children, and they all can become friends. It doesn't happen often, but when it does it is as beautiful to watch as the dawn of a new day.

Living Faithfully in an Ambiguous World

Our hearts and minds desire clarity. We like to have a clear picture of a situation, a clear view of how things fit together, and clear insight into our own and the world's problems. But just as in nature colors and shapes mingle without clear-cut distinctions, human life doesn't offer the clarity we are looking for. The borders between love and hate, evil and good, beauty and ugliness, heroism and cowardice, care and neglect, guilt and blamelessness are mostly vague, ambiguous, and hard to discern.

It is not easy to live faithfully in a world full of ambiguities. We have to learn to make wise choices without needing to be entirely sure.

Where Mourning and Dancing Touch Each Other

"[There is] a time for mourning, a time for dancing" (Ecclesiastes 3:4). But mourning and dancing are never fully separated. Their times do not necessarily follow each other. In fact, their times may become one time. Mourning may turn into dancing and dancing into mourning without showing a clear point where one ends and the other starts.

Often our grief allows us to choreograph our dance while our dance creates the space for our grief. We lose a beloved friend, and in the midst of our tears we discover an unknown joy. We celebrate a success, and in the midst of the party we feel deep sadness. Mourning and dancing, grief and laughter, sadness and gladness—they belong together as the sad-faced clown and the happy-faced clown, who make us both cry and laugh. Let's trust that the beauty of our lives becomes visible where mourning and dancing touch each other.

The Autumn of Life

The autumn leaves can dazzle us with their magnificent colors: deep red, purple, yellow, gold, bronze, in countless variations and combinations. Then, shortly after having shown their unspeakable beauty, they fall to the ground and die. The barren trees remind us that winter is near. Likewise, the autumn of life has the potential to be very colorful: wisdom, humor, care, patience, and joy may bloom splendidly just before we die.

As we look at the barren trees and remember those who have died, let us be grateful for the beauty we saw in them and wait hopefully for a new spring.

Smiles Breaking Through Tears

Dying is a gradual diminishing and final vanishing over the horizon of life. When we watch a sailboat leaving port and moving toward the horizon, it becomes smaller and smaller until we can no longer see it. But we must trust that someone is standing on a faraway shore seeing that same sailboat become larger and larger until it reaches its new harbor. Death is a painful loss. When we return to our homes after a burial, our hearts are in grief. But when we think about the One standing at the other shore eagerly waiting to welcome our beloved friend into a new home, a smile can break through our tears.

Traveling with the Eyes of God

Traveling—seeing new sights, hearing new music, and meeting new people—is exciting and exhilarating. But when we have no home to return to where someone will ask us, "How was your trip?" we might be less eager to go. Traveling is joyful when we travel with the eyes and ears of those who love us, who want to see our slides and hear our stories.

This is what life is about. It is being sent on a trip by a loving God, who is waiting at home for our return and is eager to watch the slides we took and hear about the friends we made. When we travel with the eyes and ears of the God who sent us, we will see wonderful sights, hear wonderful sounds, meet wonderful people . . . and be happy to return home.

APRIL

❦

. . . .

The Beauty of Shyness

There is something beautiful about shyness, even though in our culture shyness is not considered a virtue. On the contrary, we are encouraged to be direct, look people straight in the eyes, tell them what is on our minds, and share our stories without a blush.

But this unflinching soul-baring, confessional attitude quickly becomes boring. It is like trees without shadows. Shy people have long shadows, where they keep much of their beauty hidden from intruders' eyes. Shy people remind us of the mystery of life that cannot be simply explained or expressed. They invite us to reverent and respectful friendships and to a wordless being together in love.

The Dignity to Give and Receive

"Nobody is so poor that he or she has nothing to give, and nobody is so rich that he or she has nothing to receive." These words by Pope John Paul II offer a powerful direction for all who want to work for peace. No peace is thinkable as long as the world remains divided into two groups: those who give and those who receive. Real human dignity is found in giving as well as receiving. This is true not only for individuals but for nations, cultures, and religious communities as well.

A true vision of peace sees a continuous mutuality between giving and receiving. Let's never give anything without asking ourselves what we are receiving from those to whom we give, and let's never receive anything without asking what we have to give to those from whom we receive.

The Importance of Receiving

Receiving is often harder than giving. Giving is very important: giving insight, giving hope, giving courage, giving advice, giving support, giving money, and most of all, giving ourselves. Without giving there is no brotherhood and sisterhood.

But receiving is just as important, because by receiving we reveal to the givers that they have gifts to offer. When we say, "Thank you, you gave me hope; thank you, you gave me a reason to live; thank you, you allowed me to realize my dream," we make givers aware of their unique and precious gifts. Sometimes it is only in the eyes of the receivers that givers discover their gifts.

Daring to Become Dependent

When someone gives us a watch but we never wear it, that watch is not really received. When someone offers us an idea but we do not respond to it, that idea is not truly received. When someone introduces us to a friend but we ignore him or her, that friend does not feel well received.

Receiving is an art. It means allowing the other to become part of our lives. It means daring to become dependent on the other. It asks for the inner freedom to say, "Without you I wouldn't be who I am." Receiving with the heart is, therefore, a gesture of humility and love. So many people have been deeply hurt because their gifts were not well received. Let us be good receivers.

Deeply Rooted in God

Trees that grow tall have deep roots. Great height without great depth is dangerous. The great leaders of this world— such as St. Francis, Gandhi, and Martin Luther King, Jr.,— were all people who could live with public notoriety, influence, and power in a humble way because of their deep spiritual rootedness.

Without deep roots we easily let others determine who we are. But as we cling to our popularity, we may lose our true sense of self. Our clinging to the opinions of others reveals how superficial we are. We have little to stand on. We have to be kept alive by adulation and praise. Those who are deeply rooted in the love of God can enjoy human praise without being attached to it.

Being Humble *and* Confident

As we look at the stars and let our minds wander into the many galaxies, we come to feel so small and insignificant that anything we do, say, or think seems completely useless. But if we look into our souls and let our minds wander into the endless galaxies of our interior lives, we become so tall and significant that everything we do, say, or think appears to be of great importance.

We have to keep looking both ways to remain humble *and* confident, humorous *and* serious, playful *and* responsible. Yes, the human being is very small and very tall. It is the tension between the two that keeps us spiritually awake.

Friends as Reminders of Our Truth

Sometimes our sorrow overwhelms us so much that we no longer can believe in joy. Life just seems a cup filled to the brim with war, violence, rejection, loneliness, and endless disappointments.

At times like this we need our friends to remind us that crushed grapes can produce delicious wine. It might be hard for us to trust that any joy can come from our sorrow, but when we start taking steps in the direction of our friends' advice, even when we are not yet able to feel the truth of what they say, the joy that seemed to be lost may be found again and our sorrow may become livable.

From Blaming to Forgiving

Our most painful suffering often comes from those who love us and those we love. The relationships between husband and wife, parents and children, brothers and sisters, teachers and students, pastors and parishioners—these are where our deepest wounds occur. Even late in life, yes, even after those who wounded us have long since died, we might still need help to sort out what happened in these relationships.

The great temptation is to keep blaming those who were closest to us for our present condition, saying, "You made me who I am now, and I hate who I am." The great challenge is to acknowledge our hurts and claim our true selves as being more than the result of what other people do to us. Only when we can claim our God-made selves as the true source of our being will we be free to forgive those who have wounded us.

Being Handed Over to Suffering

People who live close together can be sources of great sorrow for one another. When Jesus chose his twelve apostles, Judas was one of them. Judas is called a traitor. A traitor, according to the literal meaning of the Greek word for "betraying," is someone who hands the other over to suffering.

The truth is that we all have something of the traitor in us because each of us hands our fellow human beings over to suffering somehow, somewhere, mostly without intending or even knowing it. Many children, even grown-up children, can experience deep anger toward their parents for having protected them too much or too little. When we are willing to confess that we often hand those we love over to suffering, even against our best intentions, we will be more ready to forgive those who, mostly against their will, are the causes of our pain.

Loving Our Religious Leaders

Religious leaders, priests, ministers, rabbis, and imams can be admired and revered but also hated and despised. We expect that our religious leaders will bring us closer to God through their prayers, teaching, and guidance. Therefore, we watch their behavior carefully and listen critically to their words. But precisely because we expect them, often without fully realizing it, to be superhuman, we are easily disappointed or even feel betrayed when they prove to be just as human as we are. Thus, our unmitigated admiration quickly turns into unrestrained anger.

Let's try to love our religious leaders, forgive them their faults, and see them as brothers and sisters. Then we will enable them, in their brokenness, to lead us closer to the heart of God.

Authority and Obedience

Authority and obedience can never be divided, with some people having all the authority while others have only to obey. This separation causes authoritarian behavior on the one side and doormat behavior on the other. It perverts authority as well as obedience. A person with great authority who has nobody to be obedient to is in great spiritual danger. A very obedient person who has no authority over anyone is equally in danger.

Jesus spoke with great authority, but his whole life was complete obedience to his Father, and Jesus, who said to his Father, "Let it be as you, not I, would have it" (Matthew 26:39), has been given all authority in heaven and on earth (see Matthew 28:18). Let us ask ourselves: Do we live our authority in obedience and do we live our obedience with authority?

❦

The Authority of Compassion

We usually think of people with great authority as higher up, far away, hard to reach. But spiritual authority comes from compassion and emerges from deep inner solidarity with those who are "subject" to authority. The one who is fully like us, who deeply understands our joys and pains or hopes and desires, and who is willing and able to walk with us, that is the one to whom we gladly give authority and whose "subjects" we are willing to be.

It is compassionate authority that empowers, encourages, calls forth hidden gifts, and enables great things to happen. True spiritual authority is located in the point of an upside-down triangle, supporting and holding into the light everyone they offer their leadership to.

The Shepherd and the Sheep

Spiritual leadership is the leadership of the Good Shepherd. As Jesus says, good shepherds know their sheep, and their sheep know them (see John 10:14). There must be a true mutuality between shepherds and sheep. Good leaders know their own, and their own know them. Between them is mutual trust, mutual openness, mutual care, and mutual love. To follow our leaders we cannot be afraid of them, and to lead our followers we need their encouragement and support.

Jesus calls himself the Good Shepherd to show the great intimacy that must exist between leaders and those entrusted to them. Without such intimacy, leadership easily becomes oppressive.

Laying Down Our Lives
for Our Friends

Good shepherds are willing to lay down their lives for their sheep (see John 10:11). As spiritual leaders walking in the footsteps of Jesus, we are called to lay down our lives for our people. This laying down might in special circumstances mean dying for others. But it means first of all making our own lives—our sorrows and joys, our despair and hope, our loneliness and experience of intimacy—available to others as sources of new life.

One of the greatest gifts we can give others is ourselves. We offer consolation and comfort, especially in moments of crisis, when we say, "Do not be afraid, I know what you are living and I am living it with you. You are not alone." Thus, we become Christ-like shepherds.

❧

Reading Spiritually About Spiritual Things

Reading often means gathering information, acquiring new insight and knowledge, and mastering a new field. It can lead us to degrees, diplomas, and certificates. Spiritual reading, however, is different. It means not simply reading about spiritual things but also reading about spiritual things in a spiritual way. That requires a willingness not just to read but to be read, not just to master but to be mastered by words. As long as we read the Bible or a spiritual book simply to acquire knowledge, our reading does not help us in our spiritual lives. We can become very knowledgeable about spiritual matters without becoming truly spiritual people.

As we read spiritually about spiritual things, we open our hearts to God's voice. Sometimes we must be willing to put down the book we are reading and just listen to what God is saying to us through its words.

Letting the Word Become Flesh

Spiritual reading is food for our souls. As we slowly let the words of the Bible or a good spiritual book enter into our minds and descend into our hearts, we become different people. The Word gradually becomes flesh in us and transforms our whole beings. Thus spiritual reading is a continuing incarnation of the divine Word within us. In and through Jesus, the Christ, God became flesh long ago. In and through our reading of God's Word and our reflection on it, God becomes flesh in us now and makes us into living Christs for today.

Let's keep reading God's Word with love and great reverence.

Growing into Our True Freedom

True freedom is the freedom of the children of God. To reach that freedom requires a lifelong discipline since so much in our world militates against it. The political, economic, social, and even religious powers surrounding us all want to keep us in bondage so that we will obey their commands and be dependent on their rewards.

But the spiritual truth that leads to freedom is the truth that we belong not to the world but to God, whose beloved children we are. By living lives in which we keep returning to that truth in word and deed, we will gradually grow into our true freedom.

The Spirit Will Speak in Us

When we are spiritually free, we do not have to worry about what to say or do in unexpected, difficult circumstances. When we are not concerned about what others think of us or what we will get for what we do, the right words and actions will emerge from the center of our beings because the Spirit of God, who makes us children of God and sets us free, will speak and act through us. Jesus says, "When you are handed over, do not worry about how to speak or what to say; what you are to say will be given to you when the time comes, because it is not you who will be speaking; the Spirit of your Father will be speaking in you" (Matthew 10:19–20).

Let's keep trusting the Spirit of God living within us, so that we can live freely in a world that keeps handing us over to judges and evaluators.

Freedom Attracts

When you are interiorly free you call others to freedom, whether you know it or not. Freedom attracts wherever it appears. A free man or a free woman creates a space where others feel safe and want to dwell. Our world is so full of conditions, demands, requirements, and obligations that we often wonder what is expected of us. But when we meet a truly free person, there are no expectations, only an invitation to reach into ourselves and discover there our own freedom.

Where true inner freedom is, there is God. And where God is, there we want to be.

Healing Contradictions

The many contradictions in our lives—such as being home while feeling homeless, being busy while feeling bored, being popular while feeling lonely, being believers while feeling many doubts—can frustrate, irritate, and even discourage us. They make us feel that we are never fully present. Every door that opens for us makes us see how many more doors are closed.

But there is another response. These same contradictions can bring us into touch with a deeper longing for the fulfillment of a desire that lives beneath all desires and that only God can satisfy. Contradictions, thus understood, create the friction that can help us move toward God.

Ordering Our Desires

Desire is often talked about as something we ought to overcome. Still, being is desiring: our bodies, our minds, our hearts, and our souls are full of desires. Some are unruly, turbulent, and very distracting; some make us think deep thoughts and see great visions; some teach us how to love; and some keep us searching for God. Our desire for God is the desire that should guide all other desires. Otherwise our bodies, minds, hearts, and souls become one another's enemies and our inner lives become chaotic, leading us to despair and self-destruction.

Spiritual disciplines are not ways to eradicate all our desires but ways to order them so that they can serve one another and together serve God.

Going Beyond Our Wants

Sometimes we behave like children in a toy shop. We want this, and that, and then something else. The many options confuse us and create an enormous restlessness in us. When someone says, "Well, what do you want? You can have one thing. Make up your mind," we do not know what to choose.

As long as our hearts keep vacillating among these many wants, we cannot move forward in life with inner peace and joy. That is why we need inner and outer disciplines, to go beyond these wants and discover our mission in life.

Being Sent into the World

Each of us has a mission in life. Jesus prays to his Father for his followers, saying, "As you sent me into the world, I have sent them into the world" (John 17:18).

We seldom realize fully that we are sent to fulfill God-given tasks. We act as if *we* have to choose how, where, and with whom to live. We act as if we were simply dropped down in creation and have to decide how to entertain ourselves until we die. But we were sent into the world by God, just as Jesus was. Once we start living our lives with that conviction, we will soon know what we were sent to do.

Fulfilling a Mission

When we live our lives as missions, we become aware that there is a home from which we are sent and to which we have to return. We start thinking about ourselves as people who are in a faraway country to bring a message or work on a project, but only for a certain amount of time. When the message has been delivered and the project is finished, we want to return home to give an account of our mission and to rest from our labors.

One of the most important spiritual disciplines is to develop the knowledge that the years of our lives are years "on a mission."

The Answers to Our Questions

We spend a lot of time and energy raising questions. Is it worth it? It is always good to ask ourselves why we raise a question. Do we want to get useful information? Do we want to show that someone else is wrong? Do we want to conquer knowledge? Do we want to grow in wisdom? Do we want to find a way to sanctity?

When we ponder *these* questions before asking *our* questions, we may discover that we need less time and energy for our questions. Perhaps we already have the information. Perhaps we don't need to show that someone is wrong. For many questions we may learn that we already have the answers, if we just listen carefully to our own hearts.

Question from Above

What are spiritual questions? They are questions from above. Most questions people ask of Jesus are questions from below, such as the question about which of a woman's seven husbands she will be married to in the resurrection. Jesus does not answer this question because it comes from a legalistic mind-set. It is a question from below.

Often Jesus responds by changing this question. In the case of the woman with seven husbands he says, "At the resurrection men and women do not marry . . . have you never read what God himself said to you: 'I am the God of Abraham, the God of Isaac and the God of Jacob?' He is God not of the dead but of the living" (Matthew 22:23–30).

We have to keep looking for the spiritual questions if we want spiritual answers.

Writing to Save the Day

Writing can be a true spiritual discipline. Writing can help us to concentrate, to get in touch with the deeper stirrings of our hearts, to clarify our minds, to process confusing emotions, to reflect on our experiences, to give artistic expression to what we are living, and to store significant events in our memories. Writing can also be good for others who might read what we write.

Quite often a difficult, painful, or frustrating day can be "redeemed" by writing about it. By writing we can claim what we have lived and thus integrate it more fully into our journeys. Then writing can become lifesaving for us and sometimes for others too.

Writing, Opening a Deep Well

Writing is not just jotting down ideas. Often we say, "I don't know what to write. I have no thoughts worth writing down." But much good writing emerges from the process of writing itself. As we simply sit down in front of a sheet of paper and start to express in words what is on our minds or in our hearts, new ideas emerge, ideas that can surprise us and lead us to inner places we hardly knew were there.

One of the most satisfying aspects of writing is that it can open in us deep wells of hidden treasures that are beautiful for us as well as for others to see.

Making Our Lives Available to Others

One of the arguments we often use for not writing is this: "I have nothing original to say. Whatever I might say, someone else has already said it, and better than I will ever be able to." This, however, is not a good argument for not writing. Each human being is unique and original, and nobody has lived what we have lived. Furthermore, what we have lived, we have lived not just for ourselves but for others as well. Writing can be a creative and invigorating way to make our lives available to ourselves and to others.

We have to trust that our stories deserve to be told. We may discover that the better we tell our stories the better we will want to live them.

Losing and Gaining Our Lives

The great paradox of life is that those who lose their lives will gain them. This paradox becomes visible in very ordinary situations. If we cling to our friends, we may lose them, but if we are nonpossessive in our relationships, we will make many friends. If fame is what we seek and desire, it often vanishes as soon as we acquire it, but if we have no need to be known, we might be remembered long after our deaths. When we want to be in the center, we easily end up on the margins, but when we are free enough to be wherever we must be, we often find ourselves in the center.

Giving away our lives for others is the greatest of all human acts. This will gain us our lives.

MAY

❦

Friends and Their Limitations

We need friends. Friends guide us, care for us, confront us in love, console us in times of pain. Although we speak of "making friends," friends cannot be made. Friends are free gifts from God. But God gives us the friends we need when we need them if we fully trust in God's love.

Friends cannot replace God. They have limitations and weaknesses like we have. Their love is never faultless, never complete. But in their limitations they can be signposts on our journey toward the unlimited and unconditional love of God. Let's enjoy the friends God has sent on our way.

Friends and Their Unique Gifts

No two friends are the same. Each has his or her own gift for us. When we expect one friend to have all we need, we will always be hypercritical, never completely happy with what he or she does have.

One friend may offer us affection, another may stimulate our minds, another may strengthen our souls. The more able we are to receive the different gifts our friends have to give us, the more able we will be to offer our own unique but limited gifts. Thus, friendships create a beautiful tapestry of love.

The Mosaic That Shows Us the Face of God

A mosaic consists of thousands of little stones. Some are blue, some are green, some are yellow, some are gold. When we bring our faces close to the mosaic, we can admire the beauty of each stone. But as we step back from it, we can see that all these little stones reveal to us a beautiful picture, telling a story none of these stones can tell by itself.

That is what our life in community is about. Each of us is like a little stone, but together we reveal the face of God to the world. Nobody can say, "I make God visible." But others who see us together can say, "They make God visible." Community is where humility and glory touch.

❦

Signposts on the Way to God

How do we know about God's love, God's generosity, God's kindness, God's forgiveness? Through our parents, our friends, our teachers, our pastors, our spouses, our children—they all reveal God to us. But as we come to know them, we realize that each of them can reveal only a little bit of God. God's love is greater than theirs; God's goodness is greater than theirs; God's beauty is greater than theirs.

At first we may be disappointed in these people. For a while we thought that they would be able to give us all the love, goodness, and beauty we needed. But gradually we discover that they were all signposts on the way to God.

God's Generosity

God is a god of abundance, not a god of scarcity. Jesus reveals to us God's abundance when he offers so much bread to the people that there are twelve large baskets with leftover scraps (see John 6:5–15), and when he makes his disciples catch so many fish that their boat nearly sinks (see Luke 5:1–7). God doesn't give us just enough. God gives us more than enough: more bread and fish than we can eat, more love than we dared to ask for.

God is a generous giver, but we can only see and enjoy God's generosity when we love God with all of our hearts, minds, and strength. As long as we say, "I will love you, God, but first show me your generosity," we will remain distant from God and unable to experience what God truly wants to give us, which is life and life in abundance.

❧

The Temptation to Hoard

As fearful people we are inclined to develop a mind-set that makes us say, "There's not enough food for everyone, so I better be sure I save enough for myself in case of emergency," or "There's not enough knowledge for everyone to enjoy; so I'd better keep my knowledge to myself, so no one else will use it," or "There's not enough love to give to everybody, so I'd better keep my friends for myself to prevent others from taking them away from me." This is a scarcity mentality. It involves hoarding whatever we have, fearful that we won't have enough to survive. The tragedy, however, is that what you cling to ends up rotting in your hands.

Seeing the Miracle of Multiplication

The opposite of a scarcity mentality is an abundancy mentality. With an abundancy mentality we say, "There is enough for everyone, more than enough: food, knowledge, love . . . everything." With this mind-set we give away whatever we have, to whomever we meet. When we see hungry people we give them food. When we meet ignorant people we share our knowledge; when we encounter people in need of love, we offer them friendship and affection and hospitality and introduce them to our family and friends.

When we live with this mind-set, we will see the miracle that what we give away multiplies: food, knowledge, love . . . everything. There will even be many leftovers.

Sharing Freely Our Knowledge

Often we think that we do not know enough to be able to teach others. We might even become hesitant to tell others what we know, out of fear that we won't have anything left to say when we are asked for more.

This mind-set makes us anxious, secretive, possessive, and self-conscious. But when we have the courage to share freely with others all that we know, whenever they ask for it, we soon discover that we know a lot more than we thought. It is only by giving generously from the well of our knowledge that we discover how deep that well is.

❧

The Cup of Life

When the mother of James and John asks Jesus to give her sons a special place in his Kingdom, Jesus responds, "Can you drink the cup that I am going to drink?" (Matthew 20:22). "Can we drink the cup?" is the most challenging and radical question we can ask ourselves. The cup is the cup of life, full of sorrows and joys. Can we hold our cups and claim them as our own? Can we lift our cups to offer blessings to others, and can we drink our cups to the bottom as cups that bring us salvation?

Keeping this question alive in us is one of the most demanding spiritual exercises we can practice.

Holding the Cup

We all must hold the cups of our lives. As we grow older and become more fully aware of the many sorrows of life—personal failures, family conflicts, disappointments in work and social life, and the many pains surrounding us on the national and international scene—everything within and around us conspires to make us ignore, avoid, suppress, or simply deny these sorrows. "Look at the sunny side of life and make the best of it," we say to ourselves and hear others say to us. But when we want to drink the cups of our lives, we need first to *hold* them, to fully acknowledge what we are living, trusting that by not avoiding but befriending our sorrows we will discover the true joy we are looking for right in the midst of our sorrows.

Lifting the Cup

When we hold firm our cups of life, fully acknowledging their sorrows and joys, we will also be able to lift our cups in human solidarity. Lifting our cups means that we are not ashamed of what we are living, and this gesture encourages others to befriend their truth as we are trying to befriend ours. By lifting our cups and saying to one another, "To life" or "To your health," we proclaim that we are willing to look truthfully at our lives together. Thus, we can become a community of people encouraging one another to drink fully the cups that have been given to us in the conviction that they will lead us to true fulfillment.

Drinking the Cup

After firmly holding the cups of our lives and lifting them up as signs of hope for others, we have to drink them. Drinking our cups means fully appropriating and internalizing what each of us has acknowledged as *our life,* with all its unique sorrows and joys.

How do we drink our cups? We drink them as we listen in silence to the truth of our lives, as we speak in trust with friends about ways we want to grow, and as we act in deeds of service. Drinking our cups is following freely and courageously God's call and staying faithfully on the path that is ours. Thus, our life cups become the cups of salvation. When we have emptied them to the bottom, God will fill them with "water" for eternal life.

❦

Emptiness and Fullness

Emptiness and fullness at first seem complete opposites. But in the spiritual life they are not. In the spiritual life we find the fulfillment of our deepest desires by becoming empty for God.

We must empty the cups of our lives completely to be able to receive the fullness of life from God. Jesus lived this on the cross. The moment of complete emptiness and complete fullness became the same. When he had given all away to his Abba, his dear Father, he cried out, "It is fulfilled" (John 19:30). He who was lifted up on the cross was also lifted into the resurrection. He who had emptied and humbled himself was raised up and "given the name above all other names" (see Philippians 2:7–9). Let us keep listening to Jesus' question: "Can you drink the cup that I am going to drink?" (Matthew 20:22).

❧

Praying to Die Well

Many people say, "I am not afraid of death, but I am afraid of dying." This is quite understandable, since dying often means illness, pain, dependency, and loneliness.

The fear of dying is nothing to be ashamed of. It is the most human of all human fears. Jesus himself entered into that fear. In his anguish "sweat fell to the ground like great drops of blood" (Luke 22:44). How must we deal with our fear of dying? Like Jesus we must pray that we may receive special strength to make the great passage to new life. Then we can trust that God will send us an angel to comfort us, as he sent an angel to Jesus.

Dying with Grateful Hearts

We often wonder how death will occur for us. Through illness, accident, war, or a natural disaster? Will our deaths happen suddenly or gradually? There are no answers for these questions, so we really should not spend time worrying about them. We don't know how our lives will end, and this is a blessed ignorance! But there is an important question that we should consider: When our time to die comes, will we die in such a way that those we leave behind will not be devastated by grief or left with feelings of shame or guilt?

How we leave others depends largely on how we prepare ourselves for death. When we are able to die with grateful hearts, grateful to God and our families and friends, our deaths can become sources of life for others.

Making Our Deaths Gifts

How do we make our deaths gifts for others? Very often people's lives are destroyed, harmed, or permanently wounded by the deaths of their relatives or friends. We have to do whatever we can to avoid this. When *we* are near death what we say to those who are close to us, whether in spoken or in written words, is very important. When we express gratitude to them, ask forgiveness for our shortcomings and offer forgiveness for theirs, and express our sincere desire that they continue their lives without remorse but remembering the graces of our lives, then our deaths can become true gifts.

Love Will Remain

Hope and faith will both come to an end when we die. But love will remain. Love is eternal. Love comes from God and returns to God. When we die, we will lose everything that life gave us except love. The love with which we lived our lives is the life of God within us. It is the divine, indestructible core of our being. This love not only will remain but will also bear fruit from generation to generation.

When we approach death let us say to those we leave behind, "Don't let your heart be troubled. The love of God that dwells in my heart will come to you and offer you consolation and comfort."

The Breath of God Within Us

When we speak about the Holy Spirit, we speak about the breath of God breathing in us. The Greek word for "spirit" is *pneuma,* which means "breath." We are seldom aware of our breathing. It is so essential for life that we only think about it when something is wrong with it.

The Spirit of God is like our breath. God's spirit is more intimate to us than we are to ourselves. We might not often be aware of it, but without it we cannot live a "spiritual life." It is the Holy Spirit of God who prays in us, who offers us the gifts of love, forgiveness, kindness, goodness, gentleness, peace, and joy. It is the Holy Spirit who offers us the life that death cannot destroy. Let us always pray, "Come, Holy Spirit, come."

The Unfinished Business
of Forgiveness

What makes us cling to life even when it is time to "move on"? Is it our unfinished business? Sometimes we cling to life because we have not yet been able to say, "I forgive you, and I ask for your forgiveness." When we have forgiven those who have hurt us and asked forgiveness from those we have hurt, a new freedom emerges. It is the freedom to move on.

When Jesus was dying he prayed for those who had nailed him to the cross: "Father, forgive them; they do not know what they are doing" (Luke 23:34). That prayer set him free to say, "Father, into your hands I commit my spirit" (Luke 23:46).

❦

Jesus' Freedom

Jesus was truly free. His freedom was rooted in his spiritual awareness that he was the Beloved Child of God. He knew in the depth of his being that he belonged to God before he was born, that he was sent into the world to proclaim God's love, and that he would return to God after his mission was fulfilled. This knowledge gave him the freedom to speak and act without having to please the world and the power to respond to people's pains with the healing love of God. That's why the Gospels say, "Everyone in the crowd was trying to touch him because power came out of him that cured them all" (Luke 6:19).

Jesus' Compassion

Jesus is called Emmanuel, which means "God-with-us" (see Matthew 1:22–23). The great paradox of Jesus' life is that he, whose words and actions are in no way influenced by human blame or praise but are completely dependent on God's will, is more "with" us than any other human being.

Jesus' compassion, his deep feeling-with-us, is possible because his life is guided not by human respect but only by the love of his heavenly Father. Indeed, Jesus is free to love us because he is not dependent on our love.

Jesus, the Blessed One

Jesus is the Blessed One. The word *benediction*, which is the Latin form for the word *blessing*, means "to say (*dicere*) good things (*bene*)." Jesus is the Blessed One because God has spoken good things of him. Most clearly we hear God's blessing after Jesus has been baptized in the river Jordan, when "suddenly there was a voice from heaven, 'This is my Son, the Beloved; my favour rests on him'" (Matthew 3:16–17).

With this blessing Jesus starts his public ministry. And all of that ministry makes known to us that this blessing is not only for Jesus but also for all who follow him.

Jesus' Self-Portrait

Jesus says, "Blessed are the poor, the gentle, those who mourn, those who hunger and thirst for uprightness, the merciful, the pure in heart, the peacemakers, and those who are persecuted in the cause of uprightness" (Matthew 5:3–10). These words offer us a self-portrait of Jesus. Jesus is the Blessed One. And the face of the Blessed One shows poverty, gentleness, grief, hunger, and thirst for uprightness, mercy, purity of heart, a desire to make peace, and the signs of persecution.

The whole message of the Gospel is this: Become like Jesus. We have his self-portrait. When we keep that in front of our eyes, we will soon learn what it means to follow Jesus and become like him.

Jesus Is Poor

Jesus, the Blessed One, is poor. The poverty of Jesus is much more than an economic or social poverty. Jesus is poor because he freely chose powerlessness over power, vulnerability over defensiveness, dependency over self-sufficiency. As the great "Song of Christ" so beautifully expresses: "He . . . did not count equality with God something to be grasped. But he emptied himself, . . . becoming as human beings are" (Philippians 2:6–7). This is the poverty of spirit that Jesus chose to live.

Jesus calls us who are blessed as he is to live our lives with that same poverty.

Jesus Is Gentle

Jesus, the Blessed One, is gentle. Even though he speaks with great fervor and biting criticism against all forms of hypocrisy and is not afraid to attack deception, vanity, manipulation, and oppression, his heart is a gentle heart. He won't break the crushed reed or snuff the faltering wick (see Matthew 12:20). He responds to people's suffering, heals their wounds, and offers courage to the fainthearted.

Jesus came to bring good news to the poor, sight to the blind, and freedom to prisoners (see Luke 4:18–19) in all he says, and thus he reveals God's immense compassion. As his followers, we are called to that same gentleness.

Jesus Mourns

Jesus, the Blessed One, mourns. Jesus mourns when his friend Lazarus dies (see John 11:33–36); he mourns when he overlooks the city of Jerusalem, soon to be destroyed (see Luke 19:41–44). Jesus mourns over all losses and devastations that fill the human heart with pain. He grieves with those who grieve and sheds tears with those who cry.

The violence, greed, lust, and so many other evils that have distorted the face of the earth and its people cause the Beloved Son of God to mourn. We too must mourn if we hope to experience God's consolation.

Jesus Hungers and Thirsts for Uprightness

Jesus, the Blessed Child of God, hungers and thirsts for uprightness. He abhors injustice. He resists those who try to gather wealth and influence by oppression and exploitation. His whole being yearns for people to treat one another as brothers and sisters, sons and daughters of the same God.

With fervor he proclaims that the way to the Kingdom is not found in saying many prayers or offering many sacrifices but in feeding the hungry, clothing the naked, and visiting the sick and the prisoners (see Matthew 25:31–46). He longs for a just world. He wants us to live with the same hunger and thirst.

Jesus Is Merciful

Jesus, the Blessed Child of God, is merciful. Showing mercy is different from having pity. Pity connotes distance, even looking down upon. When a beggar asks for money and you give him something out of pity, you are not showing mercy. Mercy comes from a compassionate heart; it comes from a desire to be an equal. Jesus didn't want to look down on us. He wanted to become one of us and feel deeply with us.

When Jesus called the only son of the widow of Nain to life, he did so because he felt the deep sorrow of the grieving mother in his own heart (see Luke 7:11–17). Let us look at Jesus when we want to know how to show mercy to our brothers and sisters.

Jesus Is Pure of Heart

Jesus, the Beloved of God, has a pure heart. Having a pure heart means willing one thing. Jesus wanted only to do the will of his heavenly Father. Whatever Jesus did or said, he did and said it as the obedient Son of God: "What I say is what the Father has taught me; he who sent me is with me, and has not left me to myself, for I always do what pleases him" (John 8:28–29). There are no divisions in Jesus' heart, no double motives or secret intentions. In Jesus there is complete inner unity because of his complete unity with God.

Becoming like Jesus is growing into purity of heart. That purity is what gave Jesus and will give us true spiritual vision.

Jesus Is a Peacemaker

Jesus, the Blessed Child of the Father, is a peacemaker. His peace doesn't mean only absence of war. It is not simply harmony or equilibrium. His peace is the fullness of well-being, gratuitously given by God. Jesus says, "Peace I leave to you, my own peace I give you, a peace which the world cannot give, this is my gift to you" (John 14:27).

Peace is Shalom—well-being of mind, heart, and body, individually and communally. It can exist in the midst of a war-torn world, even in the midst of unresolved problems and increasing human conflicts. Jesus made that peace by giving his life for his brothers and sisters. This is no easy peace, but it is everlasting and it comes from God. Are we willing to give our lives in the service of peace?

Jesus Is Persecuted

Jesus, the favorite Child of God, is persecuted. He who is poor, gentle, mourning; he who hungers and thirsts for uprightness; he who is merciful, pure of heart, and a peacemaker is not welcome in this world. The Blessed One of God is a threat to the established order and a source of constant irritation to those who consider themselves the rulers of this world. Without accusing anyone he is considered an accuser, without condemning anyone he makes people feel guilty and ashamed, without judging anyone those who see him feel judged. In their eyes, he cannot be tolerated and needs to be destroyed, because letting him be seems like a confession of guilt.

When we strive to become like Jesus, we cannot expect always to be liked and admired. We have to be prepared to be rejected.

JUNE

❦

· ·

Jesus Is *in* the World, Not *of* It

The Beatitudes offer us a self-portrait of Jesus. At first it might seem to be a most unappealing portrait—who wants to be poor, mourning, and persecuted? Who can be truly gentle, merciful, pure in heart, a peacemaker, and always concerned about justice? Where is the realism here? Don't we have to survive in this world and use the ways of the world to do so?

Jesus shows us the way to be *in* the world without being *of* it. When we model our lives on his, a new world will open up for us. The Kingdom of Heaven will be ours, and the earth will be our inheritance. We will be comforted and have our fill; mercy will be shown to us. Yes, we will be recognized as God's children and truly see God, not just in an afterlife but here and now (see Matthew 5:3–10). That is the reward of modeling our lives on the life of Jesus!

Being Like Jesus

Very often we distance ourselves from Jesus. We say, "What Jesus knew we cannot know, and what Jesus did we cannot do." But Jesus never puts any distance between himself and us. He says, "I call you friends, because I have made known to you everything I have learnt from my Father" (John 15:15) and "In all truth I tell you, whoever believes in me will perform the same works as I do myself, and will perform even greater works" (John 14:12).

Indeed, we are called to know what Jesus knew and do what Jesus did. Do we really want that, or do we prefer to keep Jesus at arm's length?

Claiming the Identity of Jesus

When we think about Jesus as that exceptional, unusual person who lived long ago and whose life and words continue to inspire us, we might avoid the realization that Jesus wants us to be like him. Jesus himself keeps saying in many ways that he, the Beloved Child of God, came to reveal to us that we too are God's beloved children, loved with the same unconditional divine love.

John writes to his people, "You must see what great love the Father has lavished on us by letting us be called God's children—which is what we are." (1 John 3:1). This is the great challenge of the spiritual life: to claim the identity of Jesus for ourselves and to say, "We are the living Christ today!"

Being Clothed in Christ

Being a believer means being clothed in Christ. Paul says, "Every one of you that has been baptized has been clothed in Christ" (Galatians 3:26) and "Let your armour be the Lord Jesus Christ" (Romans 13:14). This being "clothed in Christ" is much more than wearing a cloak that covers our misery. It refers to a total transformation that allows us to say with Paul, "I have been crucified with Christ and yet I am alive; yet it is no longer I, but Christ living in me" (Galatians 2:20).

Thus, we are the living Christ in the world. Jesus, who is God-made-flesh, continues to reveal himself in our own flesh. Indeed, true salvation is *becoming Christ*.

God's Breath Given to Us

Being the living Christ today means being filled with the same Spirit that filled Jesus. Jesus and his Father are breathing the same breath, the Holy Spirit. The Holy Spirit is the intimate communion that makes Jesus and his Father one. Jesus says, "I am in the Father and the Father is in me" (John 14:10) and "The Father and I are one" (John 10:30). It is this unity that Jesus wants to give us. That is the gift of his Holy Spirit.

Living a spiritual life, therefore, means living in the same communion with the Father as Jesus did, and thus making God present in the world.

Joint Heirs with Christ

We continue to put ourselves down as less than Christ. Thus, we avoid the full honor as well as the full pain of the Christian life. But the Spirit that guided Jesus guides us. Paul says, "The Spirit himself joins with our spirit to bear witness that we are children of God. And if we are children, then we are heirs, heirs of God and joint-heirs with Christ" (Romans 8:16–17).

When we start living according to this truth, our lives will be radically transformed. We will not only come to know the full freedom of the children of God but also the full rejection of the world. It is understandable that we hesitate to claim the honor so as to avoid the pain. But, provided we are willing to share in Christ's suffering, we also will share in his glory (see Romans 8:17).

The Power of the Spirit

In and through Jesus we come to know God as a powerless God, who becomes dependent on us. But it is precisely in this powerlessness that God's power reveals itself. This is not the power that controls, dictates, and commands. It is the power that heals, reconciles, and unites. It is the power of the Spirit. When Jesus appeared people wanted to be close to him and touch him because "power came out of him" (Luke 6:19).

It is this power of the divine Spirit that Jesus wants to give us. The Spirit indeed empowers us and allows us to be healing presences. When we are filled with that Spirit, we cannot be other than healers.

Empowered to Speak

The Spirit that Jesus gives us empowers us to speak. Often when we are expected to speak in front of people who intimidate us, we are nervous and self-conscious. But if we live in the Spirit, we don't have to worry about what to say. We will find ourselves ready to speak when the need is there. "When they take you before . . . authorities, do not worry about how to defend yourselves or what to say, because when the time comes, the Holy Spirit will teach you what you should say" (Luke 12:11–12).

We waste much of our time in anxious preparation. Let's claim the truth that the Spirit that Jesus gave us will speak in us and speak convincingly.

Empowered to Pray

Prayer is the gift of the Spirit. Often we wonder how to pray, when to pray, and what to pray. We can become very concerned about methods and techniques of prayer. But finally it is not we who pray but the Spirit who prays in us.

Paul says, "The Spirit . . . comes to help us in our weakness, for, when we do not know how to pray properly, then the Spirit personally makes our petitions for us in groans that cannot be put into words; and he who can see into all hearts knows what the Spirit means because the prayers that the Spirit makes for God's holy people are always in accordance with the mind of God" (Romans 8:26–27). These words explain why the Spirit is called the Consoler.

Empowered to Be

Who are we? Are we what we do? Are we what others say about us? Are we the power we have? It often seems that way in our society. But the Spirit of Jesus given to us reveals our true spiritual identities. The Spirit reveals that we belong not to a world of success, fame, or power but to God. The world enslaves us with fear; the Spirit frees us from that slavery and restores us to the true relationship. That is what Paul means when he says, "All who are guided by the Spirit of God are sons [daughters] of God, for what you received was not the spirit of slavery to bring you back into fear; you received the spirit of adoption, enabling us to cry out, 'Abba, Father!'" (Romans 8:15).

Who are we? We are God's beloved sons and daughters!

Empowered to
Call God "Abba"

Calling God "Abba, Father" is different from giving God a familiar name. Calling God "Abba" is entering into the same intimate, fearless, trusting, and empowering relationship with God that Jesus had. This relationship is called Spirit, and this Spirit is given to us by Jesus and enables us to cry out with him, "Abba, Father."

Calling God "Abba, Father" (see Romans 8:15; Galatians 4:6) is a cry of the heart, a prayer welling up from our innermost beings. It has nothing to do with naming God but everything to do with claiming God as the source of who we are. This claim does not come from any sudden insight or acquired conviction; it is the claim that the Spirit of Jesus makes in communion with our spirits. It is the claim of love.

Empowered to Receive Love

The Spirit reveals to us not only that God is "Abba, Father" but also that we belong to God as beloved children. The Spirit thus restores in us the relationship from which all other relationships derive their meaning.

Abba is a very intimate word. The best translation for it is "Daddy." The word *Abba* expresses trust, safety, confidence, belonging, and most of all, intimacy. It does not have the connotation of authority, power, and control that the word *Father* often evokes. On the contrary, Abba implies an embracing and nurturing love. This love includes and infinitely transcends all the love that comes to us from our fathers, mothers, brothers, sisters, spouses, friends, and lovers. It is the gift of the Spirit.

The Source of All Love

Without the love of our parents, sisters, brothers, spouses, lovers, and friends, we cannot live. Without love we die. Still, for many people this love comes in a very broken and limited way. It can be tainted by power plays, jealousy, resentment, vindictiveness, and even abuse. No human love is the perfect love our hearts desire, and sometimes human love is so imperfect that we can hardly recognize it as love.

In order not to be destroyed by the wounds inflicted by that imperfect human love, we must trust that the source of all love is God's unlimited, unconditional, perfect love, and that this love is not far away from us but is the gift of God's Spirit dwelling within us.

Choosing Love

How can someone ever trust in the existence of an unconditional divine love when most, if not all, of what he or she has experienced is the opposite of love—fear, hatred, violence, and abuse?

They are not condemned to be victims! There remains within them, hidden as it may seem, the possibility to choose love. Many people who have suffered the most horrendous rejections and been subject to the most cruel torture have been able to choose love. By choosing love they became witnesses not only to human resiliency but also to the divine love that transcends all human loves. Those who choose, even on a small scale, to love in the midst of hatred and fear are the people who offer true hope to our world.

❧

Small Steps of Love

How can we choose love when we have experienced so little of it? We choose love by taking small steps of love every time there is an opportunity. A smile, a handshake, a word of encouragement, a phone call, a card, an embrace, a kind greeting, a gesture of support, a moment of attention, a helping hand, a present, a financial contribution, a visit— all these are little steps toward love.

Each step is like a candle burning in the night. It does not take the darkness away, but it guides us through the darkness. When we look back after many small steps of love, we will discover that we have made a long and beautiful journey.

❧

Doing Love

Often we speak about love as if it were a feeling. But if we wait for a feeling of love before loving, we may never learn to love well. The feeling of love is beautiful and life-giving, but our loving cannot be based in that feeling. To love is to think, speak, and act according to the spiritual knowledge that we are infinitely loved by God and called to make that love visible in this world.

Mostly we *know* what the loving thing to do is. When we "do" love, even if others are not able to respond with love, we will discover that our feelings catch up with our acts.

Witnesses of Love

How do we know that we are infinitely loved by God when our immediate surroundings keep telling us that we'd better prove our right to exist?

The knowledge of being loved in an unconditional way, before the world presents us with its conditions, cannot come from books, lectures, television programs, or workshops. This spiritual knowledge comes from people who witness to God's love for us through their words and deeds. These people can be close to us but they can also live far away or may even have lived long ago. Their witness announces the truth of God's love and calls us to act in accordance with it.

We Are the Glory of God

Living a spiritual life is living a life in which our spirits and the Spirit of God bear a joint witness that we belong to God as God's beloved children (see Romans 8:16). This witness involves every aspect of our lives. Paul says, "Whatever you eat, then, or drink, and whatever else you do, do it all for the glory of God" (Romans 10:31). And *we* are the glory of God when we give full visibility to the freedom of the children of God.

When we live in communion with God's Spirit, we can only be witnesses, because wherever we go and whomever we meet, God's Spirit will manifest itself through us.

❧

The Fruit of the Spirit

How does the Spirit of God manifest itself through us? Often we think that to witness means to speak up in defense of God. This idea can make us very self-conscious. We wonder where and how we can make God the topic of our conversations and how to convince our families, friends, neighbors, and colleagues of God's presence in their lives. But this explicit missionary endeavor often comes from an insecure heart and, therefore, easily creates divisions.

The way God's Spirit manifests itself most convincingly is through its fruit: "love, joy, peace, patience, kindness, goodness, trustfulness, gentleness and self-control" (Galatians 5:22). These fruit speak for themselves. It is, therefore, always better to raise the question "How can *I* grow in the Spirit?" than the question "How can I make *others* believe in the Spirit?"

Right Living and Right Speaking

To be a witness for God is to be a living sign of God's presence in the world. What we live is more important than what we say, because the right way of living always leads to the right way of speaking. When we forgive our neighbors from our hearts, our hearts will speak forgiving words. When we are grateful, we will speak grateful words, and when we are hopeful and joyful, we will speak hopeful and joyful words.

When our words come too soon and we are not yet living what we are saying, we easily give double messages. Giving double messages—one with our words and another with our actions—makes us hypocrites. May our lives give us the right words, and may our words lead us to the right lives.

Growing into the Truth We Speak

Can we only speak when we are fully living what we are saying? If all our words had to cover all our actions, we would be doomed to permanent silence! Sometimes we are called to proclaim God's love even when we are not yet fully able to live it. Does that mean we are hypocrites? Only when our own words no longer call us to conversion. Nobody completely lives up to his or her own ideals and visions. But by proclaiming our ideals and visions with great conviction and great humility, we may gradually grow into the truth we speak. As long as we know that our lives always speak louder than our words, we can trust that our words will remain humble.

Words That Become Flesh

Words are important. Without them our actions lose meaning. And without meaning we cannot live. Words can offer perspective, insight, understanding, and vision. Words can bring consolation, comfort, encouragement, and hope. Words can take away fear, isolation, shame, and guilt. Words can reconcile, unite, forgive, and heal. Words can bring peace and joy, inner freedom and deep gratitude. Words, in short, can carry love on their wings. A word of love can be one of the greatest acts of love. That is because when our words become flesh in our own lives and the lives of others, we can change the world.

Jesus is the word made flesh. In him speaking and acting were one.

Words That Come from the Heart

Words that do not become flesh in us remain "just words." They have no power to affect our lives. If someone says, "I love you," without meaning it, such words do more harm than good. But if these same words are spoken from the heart, they can create new life.

It is important that we keep in touch with the source of our words. Our great temptation is to become "pleasers," people who say the right words to please others but whose words have no roots in their interior lives. We have to keep making sure our words are rooted in our hearts. The best way to do that is in prayerful silence.

Flesh Become Word

The word must become flesh, but the flesh also must become word. It is not enough for us, as human beings, just to live. We also must give words to what we are living. If we do not speak what we are living, our lives lose their vitality and creativity. When we see a beautiful view, we search for words to express what we are seeing. When we meet a caring person, we want to speak about that meeting. When we are sorrowful or in great pain, we need to talk about it. When we are surprised by joy, we want to announce it!

Through the word, we appropriate and internalize what we are living. The word makes our experience truly human.

꩜

Words That Create Community

The word is always a word for others. Words need to be heard. When we give words to what we are living, these words need to be received and responded to. A speaker needs a listener. A writer needs a reader.

When the flesh—the lived human experience—becomes word, community can develop. When we say, "Let me tell you what we saw. Come and listen to what we did. Sit down and let me tell you what happened to us. Wait until you hear whom we met," we call people together and make our lives into lives for others. The word brings us together and calls us into community. When the flesh becomes word, our bodies become part of a body of people.

A Courageous Life

"Have courage," we often say to one another. Courage is a spiritual virtue. The word *courage* comes from the Latin word *cor*, which means "heart." A courageous act is an act coming from the heart. A courageous word is a word arising from the heart. The heart, however, is not just the place our emotions are located. The heart is the center of our being, the center of all thoughts, feelings, passions, and decisions.

A courageous life, therefore, is a life lived from the center. It is a deeply rooted life, the opposite of a superficial life. "Have courage" therefore means "Let your center speak."

Spiritual Courage

Courage is connected with taking risks. Jumping the Grand Canyon on a motorbike, coming over Niagara Falls in a barrel, walking on a tightrope between the towers of New York's World Trade Center, or crossing the ocean in a rowboat are called courageous acts because people risk their lives by doing these things. But none of these dare-devil acts comes from the center of our being. They all come from the desire to test our physical limits and to become famous and popular.

Spiritual courage is completely different. It is following the deepest desires of our hearts at the risk of losing fame and popularity. It asks our willingness to lose our temporal lives in order to gain eternal life.

❦

Downward Mobility

The society in which we live suggests in countless ways that the way to go is up. Making it to the top, entering the limelight, breaking the record—that's what draws attention, gets us on the front page of the newspaper, and offers us the rewards of money and fame.

The way of Jesus is radically different. It is the way not of upward mobility but of downward mobility. It is going to the bottom, staying behind the sets, and choosing the last place! Why is the way of Jesus worth choosing? Because it is the way to the Kingdom, the way Jesus took, and the way that brings everlasting life.

Taking Up Our Crosses

Jesus says, "If anyone wants to be a follower of mine, let him . . . take up his cross and follow me" (Matthew 16:24). He does not say "Make a cross" or "Look for a cross." Each of us has a cross to carry. There is no need to make one or look for one. The cross we have is hard enough for us! But are we willing to take it up, to accept it as our cross?

Maybe we can't study, maybe we are handicapped, maybe we suffer from depression, maybe we experience conflict in our families, maybe we are victims of violence or abuse. We didn't choose any of it, but these things are our crosses. We can ignore them, reject them, refuse them, or hate them. But we can also take up these crosses and follow Jesus with them.

Coming Home

In the parable of the prodigal son (see Luke 15:11–32), there are two sons: the younger son, who runs away from home to an alien country, and the older son, who stays home to do his duty. The younger son dissipates himself with alcohol and sex; the older son alienates himself by working hard and dutifully fulfilling all his obligations. Both are lost. Their father grieves over both, because with neither of them does he experience the intimacy he desires.

Both lust and cold obedience can prevent us from being true children of God. Whether we are like the younger son or the older son, we have to come home to the place where we can rest in the embrace of God's unconditional love.

JULY

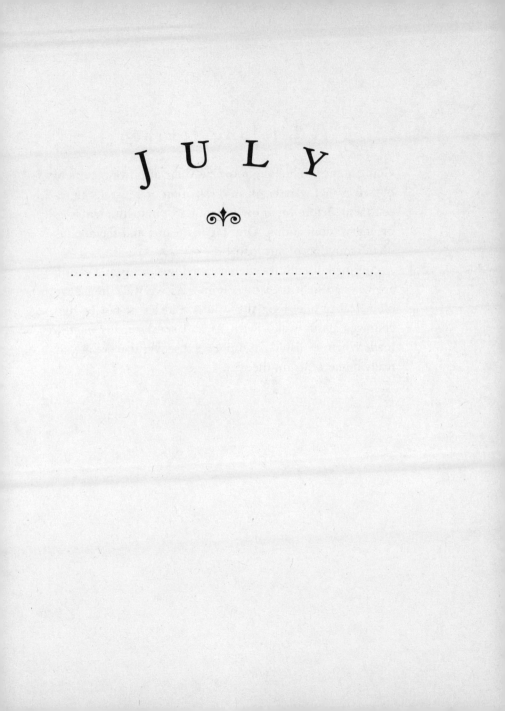

A Lifelong Journey

Going home is a lifelong journey. There are always parts of ourselves that wander off in dissipation or get stuck in resentment. Before we know it we are lost in lustful fantasies or angry ruminations. Our night dreams and daydreams often remind us of our lostness.

Spiritual disciplines such as praying, fasting, and caring are ways to help us return home. As we walk home we often realize how long the way is. But let us not be discouraged. Jesus walks with us and speaks to us on the road. When we listen carefully we discover that we are already home while on the way.

❦

Becoming Fathers and Mothers

What are we going to do when we get home? When the two sons of the parable of the prodigal son both have returned to their father, what then? The answer is simple: They have to become fathers themselves. Sons have to become fathers; daughters have to become mothers. Being children of God involves growing up and becoming like God. Jesus doesn't hesitate to say this: "Be perfect as your heavenly Father is perfect, be compassionate as your heavenly Father is compassionate" (see Matthew 5:48 and Luke 6:36). How? By welcoming home our lost brothers and sisters the way our Father welcomes us home.

Welcoming Home

How do we welcome home our lost brothers and sisters? By running out to them, embracing them, and kissing them. By clothing them with the best clothes we have and making them our honored guests. By offering them the best food and inviting friends and family for a party. And, most important of all, by not asking for excuses or explanations, only showing our immense joy that they are with us again (see Luke 15:20–24).

That is being perfect as our heavenly Father is perfect. It is forgiving from the heart without a trace of self-righteousness, recrimination, or even curiosity. The past is wiped out. What counts is the here and now, where all that fills our hearts is gratitude for the homecoming of our brothers and sisters.

The Tears of the Father

The father in the story of the prodigal son suffered much. He saw his younger son leave, knowing the disappointments, rejections, and abuses facing him. He saw his older son become angry and bitter, and was unable to offer him affection and support. A large part of the father's life had been spent waiting. He could not force his younger son to come home or his older son to let go of his resentments. Only they themselves could take the initiative to return.

During these long years of waiting the father cried many tears and died many deaths. He was emptied out by suffering. But that emptiness created a place of welcome for his sons when the time of their return came. We are called to become like that father.

A Father's As Well As a Mother's Love

The father in the story of the prodigal son is mother as well. His running out to welcome his son, his embrace and kisses; his offering of the best robe, the ring, and the sandals; and his throwing a party are not the typical behavior of a distant patriarch. They express so much tenderness, nurturing care, and self-effacing forgiveness that in them we see both motherly and fatherly love fully present.

The perfect love of our heavenly Father includes as well as transcends all the love that a father and mother can have for their children. We may think about the two hands of God embracing us as a mother's hand and a father's hand: one caressing, consoling, and comforting; the other supporting, encouraging, and empowering. We too are called to be father and mother to those who want to come home.

Beyond Jealousy

Jealousy arises easily in our hearts. In the parable of the
prodigal son, the elder son is jealous that his younger
brother gets such a royal welcome even though he and his
loose women swallowed up his father's property (see Luke
15:30). And in the parable of the laborers in the vineyard,
the workers who worked the whole day are jealous that
those who came at the eleventh hour received the same pay
as they did (see Matthew 20:1–16). But the Father says to
the older son, "You are with me always and all I have is
yours" (Luke 15:31). And the landowner says, "Why should
you be envious because I am generous?" (Matthew 20:15).

When we truly enjoy God's unlimited generosity, we
will be grateful for what our brothers and sisters receive.
Jealousy will simply have no place in our hearts.

How Time Heals

"Time heals," people often say. This is not true when it means that we will eventually forget the wounds inflicted on us and be able to live on as if nothing happened. That is not really healing; it is simply ignoring reality. But when the expression "time heals" means that faithfulness in a difficult relationship can lead us to a deeper understanding of the ways we have hurt each other, then there is much truth in it. "Time heals" implies not passively waiting but actively working with our pain and trusting in the possibility of forgiveness and reconciliation.

Wounded Healers

Nobody escapes being wounded. We all are wounded people, whether physically, emotionally, mentally, or spiritually. The main question is not "How can we hide our wounds?" so we don't have to be embarrassed but "How can we put our woundedness in the service of others?" When our wounds cease to be a source of shame and become a source of healing, we have become wounded healers.

Jesus is God's wounded healer: Through his wounds we are healed. Jesus' suffering and death brought joy and life. His humiliation brought glory; his rejection brought a community of love. As followers of Jesus we can also allow our wounds to bring healing to others.

Tending Our Own Wounds First

Our own experience with loneliness, depression, and fear can become a gift for others, especially when we have received good care. As long as our wounds are open and bleeding, we scare others away. But after someone has carefully tended to our wounds, they no longer frighten us or others.

When we experience the healing presence of another person, we can discover our own gifts of healing. Then our wounds allow us to enter into a deep solidarity with our wounded brothers and sisters.

Listening with Our Wounds

To enter into solidarity with a suffering person does not mean that we have to talk with that person about our own suffering. Speaking about our own wounds is seldom helpful to someone who is in pain. A wounded healer is someone who can listen to a person in pain without having to speak about his or her own wounds. When we have lived through a painful depression, we can listen with great attentiveness and love to a depressed friend without mentioning our experience. Mostly it is better not to direct a suffering person's attention to ourselves. We have to trust that our own bandaged wounds will allow us to listen to others with our whole being. That is healing.

A Time to Receive and a Time to Give

It is important to know when we should give attention and when we need attention. Often we are inclined to give, give, and give without asking anything in return. We may think that this is a sign of generosity or even heroism. But it might be little more than a proud attitude that says, "I don't need help from others. I only want to give." When we keep giving without receiving we burn out quickly. Only when we pay careful attention to our own physical, emotional, mental, and spiritual needs can we be, and remain, joyful givers.

There is a time to give and a time to receive. We need equal time for both if we want to live healthy lives.

Becoming Food for the World

When Jesus took bread, blessed it, broke it, and gave it to his disciples, he summarized in these gestures his own life. Jesus is chosen from all eternity, blessed at his baptism in the Jordan River, broken on the cross, and given as bread to the world. Being chosen, blessed, broken, and given is the sacred journey of the Son of God, Jesus the Christ.

When we take bread, bless it, break it, and give it with the words "This is the Body of Christ," we express our commitment to make our lives conform to the life of Christ. We too want to live as people chosen, blessed, and broken, and thus become food for the world.

Being Chosen

Jesus is taken by God or, better, chosen by God. Jesus is the Chosen One. From all eternity God has chosen his most precious Child to become the savior of the world. Being chosen expresses a special relationship, being known and loved in a unique way, being singled out. In our society our being chosen always implies that others are not chosen. But this is not true for God. God chooses his Son to reveal to us *our* chosenness.

In the Kingdom of God there is no competition or rivalry. The Son of God shares his chosenness with us. In the Kingdom of God each person is precious and unique, and each person has been given eyes to see the chosenness of others and rejoice in it.

Being Blessed

Jesus is the Blessed One. When Jesus was baptized in the
Jordan River a voice came from heaven saying, "You are
my Son, the Beloved; my favor rests on you" (Mark 1:11).
This was the blessing that sustained Jesus during his life.
Whatever happened to him—praise or blame—he clung to
his blessing; he always remembered that he was the favorite child of God.

Jesus came into the world to share that blessing with
us. He came to open our ears to the voice that also says to
us, "You are my beloved son, you are my beloved daughter,
my favor rests on you." When we can hear that voice, trust
in it, and remember it, especially during dark times, we
can live our lives as God's blessed children and find the
strength to share this blessing with others.

Being Broken

Jesus was broken on the cross. He lived his suffering and death not as an evil to avoid at all costs but as a mission to embrace. We too are broken. We live with broken bodies, broken hearts, broken minds, or broken spirits. We suffer from broken relationships.

How can we live our brokenness? Jesus invites us to embrace our brokenness as he embraced the cross and live it as part of our mission. He asks us not to reject our brokenness as a curse from God that reminds us of our sinfulness but to accept it and put it under God's blessing for our purification and sanctification. Thus, our brokenness can become a gateway to new life.

Being Given

Jesus is given to the world. He was chosen, blessed, and broken to be given. Jesus' life and death are a life and death for others. The Beloved Son of God, chosen from all eternity, was broken on the cross so that this one life could multiply and become food for people of all places and all times.

As God's beloved children we have to believe that our little lives, when lived as God's chosen and blessed children, are broken to be given to others. We too have to become bread for the world. When we live our brokenness under the blessing, our lives will continue to bear fruit from generation to generation. That is the story of the saints—they died, but they continue to be alive in the hearts of those who live after them—and this can be our story too.

❦

Becoming the Living Christ

Whenever we come together around the table, take bread, bless it, break it, and give it to one another, saying, "The Body of Christ," we know that Jesus is among us. He is among us not as a vague memory of a person who lived long ago but as a real, life-giving presence that transforms us. By eating the Body of Christ, we become the living Christ and we are enabled to discover our own chosenness and blessedness, acknowledge our brokenness, and trust that all we live we live for others. Thus, we, like Jesus himself, become food for the world.

The Body of Community

When we gather around the table and break bread together, we are transformed not only individually but also as community. We, people from different ages and races, with different backgrounds and histories, become one body. As Paul says, "As there is one loaf, so we, although there are many of us, are one single body, for we all share in the one loaf" (1 Corinthians 10:17).

Not only as individuals but also as community we become the living Christ, taken, blessed, broken, and given to the world. As one body, we become a living witness of God's immense desire to bring all peoples and nations together as the one family of God.

Recognizing Christ in Suffering Communities

Communities as well as individuals suffer. All over the world there are large groups of people who are persecuted, mistreated, abused, and made victims of horrendous crimes. There are suffering families, suffering circles of friends, suffering religious communities, suffering ethnic groups, and suffering nations. In these suffering bodies of people we must be able to recognize the suffering Christ. They too are chosen, blessed, broken, and given to the world.

As we call one another to respond to the cries of these people and work together for justice and peace, we are caring for Christ, who suffered and died for the salvation of our world.

Who Is My Neighbor?

"Love your neighbor as yourself" the Gospel says (Matthew 22:38). But who is my neighbor? We often respond to that question by saying, "My neighbors are all the people I am living with on this earth, especially the sick, the hungry, the dying, and all who are in need." But this is not what Jesus says. When Jesus tells the story of the good Samaritan (see Luke 10:29–37) to answer the question "Who is my neighbour?" he ends by asking, "Which . . . do you think, proved himself a neighbour to the man who fell into the bandits' hands?" The neighbor, Jesus makes clear, is not the poor man lying on the side of the road, stripped, beaten, and half dead, but the Samaritan who crossed the road, "bandaged his wounds, pouring oil and wine on them, . . . lifted him onto his own mount and took him to an inn and looked after him." My neighbor is the one who crosses the road for me!

Crossing the Road for One Another

We become neighbors when we are willing to cross the road for one another. There is so much separation and segregation: between black people and white people, between gay people and straight people, between young people and old people, between sick people and healthy people, between prisoners and free people, between Jews and Gentiles, Muslims and Christians, Protestants and Catholics, Greek Catholics and Latin Catholics.

There is a lot of road crossing to do. We are all very busy in our own circles. We have our own people to go to and our own affairs to take care of. But if we could cross the road once in a while and pay attention to what is happening on the other side, we might indeed become neighbors.

❧

Bridging the Gap
Between People

To become neighbors is to bridge the gap between people. As long as there is distance between us and we cannot look into one another's eyes, all sorts of false ideas and images arise. We give them names, make jokes about them, cover them with our prejudices, and avoid direct contact. We think of them as enemies. We forget that they love as we love, care for their children as we care for ours, become sick and die as we do. We forget that they are our brothers and sisters and treat them as objects that can be destroyed at will.

Only when we have the courage to cross the road and look in one another's eyes can we see there that we are children of the same God and members of the same human family.

What We Feel Is Not Who We Are

Our emotional lives move up and down constantly. Sometimes we experience great mood swings: from excitement to depression, from joy to sorrow, from inner harmony to inner chaos. A little event, a word from someone, a disappointment in work, many things can trigger such mood swings. Mostly we have little control over these changes. It seems that they happen *to* us rather than being created *by* us.

Thus, it is important to know that our emotional life is not the same as our spiritual life. Our spiritual life is the life of the Spirit of God within us. As we feel our emotions shift we must connect our spirits with the Spirit of God and remind ourselves that what we *feel* is not who we are. We are and remain, whatever our moods, God's beloved children.

Overcoming Our Mood Swings

Are we condemned to be passive victims of our moods? Must we simply say, "I feel great today" or "I feel awful today," and require others to live with our moods?

Although it is very hard to control our moods, we can gradually overcome them by living a well-disciplined spiritual life. This can prevent us from acting out of our moods. We might not "feel" like getting up in the morning because we "feel" that life is not worth living, that nobody loves us, and that our work is boring. But if we get up anyhow, to spend some time reading the Gospels, praying the Psalms, and thanking God for a new day, our moods may lose their power over us.

Digging into Our Spiritual Resources

When someone hurts us, offends us, ignores us, or rejects us, a deep inner protest emerges. It can be rage or depression, desire to take revenge or even an impulse to harm ourselves. We can feel a deep urge to wound those who have wounded us or to withdraw in a suicidal mood of self-rejection. Although these extreme reactions might seem exceptional, they are never far away from our hearts. During the long nights we often find ourselves brooding about words and actions we might have used in response to what others have said or done to us.

It is precisely here that we have to dig deep into our spiritual resources and find the center within us, the center that lies beyond our need to hurt others or ourselves, where we are free to forgive and love.

The Dynamics of the Spiritual Life

Our emotional lives and our spiritual lives have different dynamics. The ups and downs of our emotional lives depend a great deal on our past or present surroundings. We are happy, sad, angry, bored, excited, depressed, loving, caring, hateful, or vengeful because of what happened long ago or what is happening now.

The ups and downs of our spiritual lives depend on our obedience—that is, our attentive listening—to the movements of the Spirit of God within us. Without this listening our spiritual life eventually becomes subject to the windswept waves of our emotions.

A Window on Our Spiritual Lives

Even though our emotional and spiritual lives are distinct, they do influence one another profoundly. Our feelings often give us a window on our spiritual journeys. When we cannot let go of jealousy, we may wonder if we are in touch with the Spirit in us that cries out "Abba." When we feel very peaceful and "centered," we may come to realize that this is a sign of our deep awareness of our belovedness.

Likewise our prayer lives, lived as faithful response to the presence of the Spirit within us, may open a window on our emotions, feelings, and passions and give us some indication of how to put them in the service of our long journey into the heart of God.

❧

Putting Our Temperaments in the Service of God

Our temperaments—whether flamboyant, phlegmatic, introverted, or extroverted—are quite permanent fixtures of our personalities. Still, the way we "use" our temperaments on a daily basis can vary greatly. When we are attentive to the Spirit of God within us, we will gradually learn to put our temperaments in the service of a virtuous life. Then flamboyance gives great zeal for the Kingdom, phlegmatism helps to keep an even keel in times of crisis, introversion deepens the contemplative side, and extroversion encourages creative ministry.

Let's live with our temperaments as with gifts that help us deepen our spiritual lives.

Spiritual Dryness

Sometimes we experience a terrible dryness in our spiritual lives. We feel no desire to pray, don't experience God's presence, get bored with worship services, and even think that everything we ever believed about God, Jesus, and the Holy Spirit is little more than a childhood fairy tale.

Then it is important to realize that most of these feelings and thoughts are just feelings and thoughts, and that the Spirit of God dwells beyond our feelings and thoughts. It is a great grace to be able to experience God's presence in our feelings and thoughts, but when we don't, it does not mean that God is absent. It often means that God is calling us to a greater faithfulness. It is precisely in times of spiritual dryness that we must hold on to our spiritual discipline so that we can grow into new intimacy with God.

Two Kinds of Loneliness

In the spiritual life we have to make a distinction between two kinds of loneliness. In the first loneliness, we are out of touch with God and experience ourselves as anxiously looking for someone or something that can give us a sense of belonging, intimacy, and home. The second loneliness comes from an intimacy with God that is deeper and greater than our feelings and thoughts can capture.

We might think of these two kinds of loneliness as two forms of blindness. The first blindness comes from the absence of light, the second from too much light. The first loneliness we must try to outgrow with faith and hope. The second we must be willing to embrace in love.

Jesus' Loneliness

When Jesus came close to his death, he no longer could experience God's presence. He cried out, "My God, my God, why have you forsaken me?" (Matthew 27:47). Still, in love he held on to the truth that God was with him and said, "Father, into your hands I commit my spirit" (Luke 23:46).

The loneliness of the cross led Jesus to the resurrection. As we grow older we are often invited by Jesus to follow him into this loneliness, the loneliness in which God is too close to be experienced by our limited hearts and minds. When this happens, let us pray for the grace to surrender our spirits to God as Jesus did.

AUGUST

❧

All People Lifted Up with Jesus

The death and resurrection of Jesus are God's way to open for all people the door to eternal life. Jesus said, "When I am lifted up from the earth, I shall draw all people to myself" (John 12:32). Indeed, all people, from all times and places, are lifted up with Jesus on the cross and into the new life of the resurrection. Thus, Jesus' death is a death for all humanity, and Jesus' resurrection is a resurrection for all humanity.

Not one person from the past, present, or future is excluded from the great passage of Jesus from slavery to freedom, from the land of captivity to the promised land, from death to eternal life.

Jesus Takes Away Fatality

The great mystery of the incarnation is that God became human in Jesus so that all human flesh could be clothed with divine life. Our lives are fragile and destined to death. But since God, through Jesus, shared in our fragile and mortal lives, death no longer has the final word. Life has become victorious. Paul writes, "And after this perishable nature has put on imperishability and this mortal nature has put on immortality, then will the words of scripture come true: 'Death is swallowed up in victory. Death, where is your victory? Death, where is your sting?'" (1 Corinthians 15:54). Jesus has taken away the fatality of our existence and given our lives eternal value.

The Door Open to Anyone

Jesus is the door to a life in and with God. "I am the gate," he says (John 10:9). "I am the Way; I am Truth and Life. No one can come to the Father except through me" (John 14:6). Still, many people never have heard or will hear of Jesus. They are born, live their lives, and die without having been exposed to Jesus and his words. Are they lost? Is there no place in the Father's house for them?

Jesus opened the door to God's house for all people, also for those who never knew or will know that it was Jesus who opened it. The Spirit that Jesus sent "blows where it pleases" (John 3:8), and it can lead anyone through the door to God's house.

Jesus Comes to Us in the Poor

What finally counts is not whether we know Jesus and his words but whether we live our lives in the Spirit of Jesus. The Spirit of Jesus is the Spirit of Love. Jesus himself makes this clear when he speaks about the last judgment. There people will ask, "Lord, when did we see you hungry and feed you, or thirsty and give you drink?" and Jesus will answer, "In so far as you did this to one of the least . . . of mine, you did it to me" (Matthew 25:37, 40).

This is our great challenge and consolation. Jesus comes to us in the poor, the sick, the dying, the prisoners, the lonely, the disabled, the rejected. There we meet him, and there the door to God's house is opened for us.

Sharing the Abundant Love

Why must we go out to the far ends of the world to preach the Gospel of Jesus when people do not have to know Jesus in order to enter the house of God? We must go out because we want to share with all people the abundant love and hope, joy and peace that Jesus brought to us. We want to "proclaim the unfathomable treasure of Christ" and "throw light on the inner workings of the mystery kept hidden through all ages in God, the creator of everything" (Ephesians 3:8–9).

What we have received is so beautiful and so rich that we cannot hold it for ourselves but feel compelled to bring it to every human being we meet.

Being Joyful Witnesses

To speak about Jesus and his divine work of salvation shouldn't be a burden or a heavy obligation. When we go to people feeling that unless they accept our way of knowing Jesus, *they* are lost and *we* are failures, it is hardly possible to be true witnesses.

It is a great joy when people recognize through our witness that Jesus is the divine redeemer who opened for them the way to God. It is a true cause for gratitude and celebration. But we should also be able to live joyful and grateful lives when our witness with deeds and words does not lead people to accept Jesus in the way we do.

Keeping the Peace in Our Hearts

Whatever we do in the Name of Jesus, we must always keep the peace of Jesus in our hearts. When Jesus sends his disciples out to preach the Gospel he says, "Whatever town or village you go into, seek out someone worthy and stay with him until you leave. As you enter his house, salute it, and if the house deserves it, may your peace come upon it; if it does not, may your peace come back to you" (Matthew 10:11–13).

The great temptation is to let people take our peace away. This happens whenever we become angry, hostile, bitter, spiteful, manipulative, or vengeful when others do not respond favorably to the good news we bring to them.

Being Unconditional Witnesses

Good news becomes bad news when it is announced without peace and joy. Anyone who proclaims the forgiving and healing love of Jesus with a bitter heart is a false witness. Jesus is the savior of the world. We are not. We are called to witness, always with our lives and sometimes with our words, to the great things God has done for us. But this witness must come from a heart that is willing to give without getting anything in return.

The more we trust in God's unconditional love for us, the more able we will be to proclaim the love of Jesus without any inner or outer conditions.

Being Living Signs of Love

Jesus' whole life was a witness to his Father's love, and Jesus calls his followers to carry on that witness in his Name. We, as followers of Jesus, are sent into this world to be visible signs of God's unconditional love. Thus, we are judged not first of all by what we say but by what we live. When people say of us, "See how they love one another," they catch a glimpse of the Kingdom of God that Jesus announced and are drawn to it as by a magnet.

In a world so torn apart by rivalry, anger, and hatred, we have the privileged vocation to be living signs of a love that can bridge all divisions and heal all wounds.

Burning with Love

Often we are preoccupied with the question "How can we be witnesses in the Name of Jesus? What are we supposed to say or do to make people accept the love that God offers them?" These questions are expressions more of our fear than of our love. Jesus shows us the way of being witnesses. He was so full of God's love, so connected with God's will, so burning with zeal for God's Kingdom, that he couldn't do other than witness. Wherever he went and whomever he met, a power went out from him that healed everyone who touched him (see Luke 6:19).

If we want to be witnesses like Jesus, our only concern should be to be as alive with the love of God as Jesus was.

Trusting in the Fruits

We belong to a generation that wants to see the results of our work. We want to be productive and see with our own eyes what we have made. But that is not the way of God's Kingdom. Often our witness for God does not lead to tangible results. Jesus himself died as a failure on a cross. There was no success there to be proud of. Still, the fruitfulness of Jesus' life is beyond any human measure. As faithful witnesses of Jesus we have to trust that our lives too will be fruitful, even though we cannot see their fruit. The fruit of our lives may be visible only to those who live after us.

What is important is how well we love. God will make our love fruitful, whether we see that fruitfulness or not.

The Hidden Life of Jesus

The largest part of Jesus' life was hidden. Jesus lived with his parents in Nazareth, "under their authority" (Luke 2:51), and there "increased in wisdom, in stature, and in favour with God and with people" (Luke 2:52). When we think about Jesus we mostly think about his words and miracles, his passion, death, and resurrection, but we should never forget that before all of that Jesus lived a simple, hidden life in a small town, far away from all the great people, great cities, and great events. Jesus' hidden life is very important for our own spiritual journeys. If we want to follow Jesus by words and deeds in the service of his Kingdom, we must first of all strive to follow Jesus in his simple, unspectacular, and very ordinary hidden life.

Hiddenness, a Place of Intimacy

Hiddenness is an essential quality of the spiritual life. Solitude, silence, ordinary tasks, being with people without great agendas, sleeping, eating, working, playing . . . all of that without being different from others, that is the life that Jesus lived and the life he asks us to live. It is in hiddenness that we, like Jesus, can increase "in wisdom, in stature, and in favour with God and with people" (Luke 2:52). It is in hiddenness that we can find a true intimacy with God and a true love for people.

Even during his active ministry, Jesus continued to return to hidden places to be alone with God. If we don't have a hidden life with God, our public life for God cannot bear fruit.

Hiddenness, a Place of Purification

One of the reasons that hiddenness is such an important aspect of the spiritual life is that it keeps us focused on God. In hiddenness we do not receive human acclamation, admiration, support, or encouragement. In hiddenness we have to go to God with our sorrows and joys and trust that God will give us what we most need.

In our society we are inclined to avoid hiddenness. We want to be seen and acknowledged. We want to be useful to others and influence the course of events. But as we become visible and popular, we grow dependent on people and their responses and easily lose touch with God, the true source of our being. Hiddenness is the place of purification. In hiddenness we find our true selves.

Protecting Our Hiddenness

If indeed the spiritual life is essentially a hidden life, how do we protect this hiddenness in the midst of a very public life? The two most important ways to protect our hiddenness are found in solitude and poverty. Solitude allows us to be alone with God. There we experience that we belong not to people, not even to those who love us and care for us, but to God and God alone. Poverty is where we experience our own and other people's weaknesses, limitations, and need for support. To be poor is to be without success, without fame, and without power. But there God chooses to show us God's love.

Both solitude and poverty protect the hiddenness of our lives.

Clinging to God in Solitude

When we enter into solitude to be alone with God, we quickly discover how dependent we are. Without the many distractions of our daily lives, we feel anxious and tense. When nobody speaks to us, calls on us, or needs our help, we start feeling like nobodies. Then we begin wondering whether we are useful, valuable, or significant. Our tendency is to leave this fearful solitude quickly and get busy again to reassure ourselves that we are "somebodies." But that is a temptation, because what makes us somebodies is not other people's responses to us but God's eternal love for us.

To claim the truth of ourselves we have to cling to our God in solitude as to the One who makes us who we are.

Focusing Our Minds
and Hearts

How can we stay in solitude when we feel that deep urge to be distracted by people and events? The most simple way is to focus our minds and hearts on a word or picture that reminds us of God. By repeating quietly, "The Lord is my shepherd, there is nothing I shall want," or by gazing lovingly at an icon of Jesus, we can bring our restless minds to some rest and experience a gentle divine presence.

This doesn't happen overnight. It asks a faithful practice. But when we spend a few moments every day just being with God, our endless distractions will gradually disappear.

❦

Our Poverty,
God's Dwelling Place

How can we embrace poverty as a way to God when everyone around us wants to become rich? Poverty has many forms. We have to ask ourselves, "What is my poverty?" Is it lack of money, lack of emotional stability, lack of a loving partner, lack of security, lack of safety, lack of self-confidence? Each human being has a place of poverty. That's the place where God wants to dwell! "How blessed are the poor," Jesus says (Matthew 5:3). This means that our blessing is hidden in our poverty.

We are so inclined to cover up our poverty and ignore it that we often miss the opportunity to discover God, who dwells in it. Let's dare to see our poverty as the land in which our treasure is hidden.

Meeting God in the Poor

When we are not afraid to confess our own poverty, we will be able to be with other people in theirs. The Christ who lives in our own poverty recognizes the Christ who lives in other people's. Just as we are inclined to ignore our own poverty, we are inclined to ignore others'. We prefer not to see people who are destitute, we do not like to look at people who are deformed or disabled, we avoid talking about people's pains and sorrows, we stay away from brokenness, helplessness, and neediness.

By this avoidance we might lose touch with the people through whom God is manifested to us. But when we have discovered God in our own poverty, we will lose our fear of the poor and go to them to meet God.

The Treasure of the Poor

The poor have a treasure to offer precisely because they cannot return our favors. By not paying us for what we have done for them, they call us to inner freedom, selflessness, generosity, and true care. Jesus says, "When you have a party, invite the poor, the crippled, the lame, the blind; then you will be blessed, for they have no means to repay you and so you will be repaid when the upright rise again" (Luke 14:13–14).

The repayment Jesus speaks about is spiritual. It is the joy, peace, and love of God that we so much desire. This is what the poor give us, not only in the afterlife but already here and now.

Taking the Sting out of Death

Dying is returning home. But even though we have been told this many times by many people, we seldom desire to return home. We prefer to stay where we are. We know what we have; we do not know what we will get. Even the most appealing images of the afterlife cannot take away the fear of dying. We cling to life, even when our relationships are difficult, our economic circumstances harsh, and our health quite poor.

Still, Jesus came to take the sting out of death and to help us gradually realize that we don't have to be afraid of death, since death leads us to the place where the deepest desires of our hearts will be satisfied. It is not easy for us to truly believe that, but every little gesture of trust will bring us closer to this truth.

Living Our Passages Well

Death is a passage to new life. That sounds very beautiful, but few of us desire to make this passage. It might be helpful to realize that our final passage is preceded by many earlier passages. When we are born we make a passage from life in the womb to life in the family. When we go to school we make a passage from life in the family to life in the larger community. When we get married we make a passage from a life with many options to a life committed to one person. When we retire we make a passage from a life of clearly defined work to a life asking for new creativity and wisdom.

Each of these passages is a death leading to new life. When we live these passages well, we are becoming more prepared for our final passage.

The Quality of Life

It is very hard to accept an early death. When friends who are seventy, eighty, or ninety years old die, we may be in deep grief and miss them very much, but we are grateful that they had long lives. But when a teenager, a young adult, or a person at the height of his or her career dies, we feel a protest rising from our hearts: "Why? Why so soon? Why so young? It is unfair."

But far more important than our quantity of years is the quality of our lives. Jesus died young. St. Francis died young. St. Thérèse of Lisieux died young. Martin Luther King, Jr., died young. We do not know how long we will live, but this not knowing calls us to live every day, every week, every year of our lives to its fullest potential.

Parents' Grief

Many parents have to suffer the death of a child, at birth or at a very young age. There probably is no greater suffering than losing a child, since it so radically interferes with the desire of a father and mother to see their child grow up to be a beautiful, healthy, mature, and loving person. The great danger is that the death of a child will take away the parents' desire to live. It requires an enormous act of faith on the part of parents to truly believe that their children, however brief their lives, were given to them as gifts from God, to deepen and enrich their own lives.

Whenever parents can make that leap of faith, their children's short lives can become fruitful far beyond their expectations.

Love and the Pain of Leaving

Every time we make the decision to love someone, we open ourselves to great suffering, because those we love most cause us not only great joy but also great pain. The greatest pain comes from leaving. When the child leaves home, when the husband or wife leaves for a long period of time or for good, when the beloved friend departs to another country or dies, the pain of the leaving can tear us apart.

Still, if we want to avoid the suffering of leaving, we will never experience the joy of loving. And love is stronger than fear, life stronger than death, hope stronger than despair. We have to trust that the risk of loving is always worth taking.

Remembering the Dead

When we lose a dear friend, someone we have loved deeply, we are left with a grief that can paralyze us emotionally for a long time. People we love become part of us. Our thinking, feeling, and acting are codetermined by them: Our fathers, our mothers, our husbands, our wives, our lovers, our children, our friends—they all are living in our hearts. When they die a part of us dies too. That is what grief is about: It is that slow and painful departure of someone who has become an intimate part of us. When Christmas, the new year, a birthday, or an anniversary comes, we feel deeply the absence of our beloved companion. We sometimes have to live a whole year or more before our hearts have fully said good-bye and the pain of our grief recedes. But as we let go of them they become part of our "members," and as we "re-member" them they become guides on our spiritual journey.

Being Ready to Die

Death often happens suddenly. A car accident, a plane crash, a fatal fight, a war, a flood, and so on. When we feel healthy and full of energy, we do not think much about our death. Still, death might come very unexpectedly.

How can we be prepared to die? By not having any unfinished relational business. The question is, Have I forgiven those who have hurt me and asked forgiveness from those I have hurt? When I feel at peace with all the people who are part of my life, my death might cause great grief, but it will not cause guilt or anger.

When we are ready to die at any moment, we are also ready to live at any moment.

A Grateful Death

When we think about death, we often think about what will happen to us after we have died. But it is more important to think about what will happen to those we leave behind. The way we die has a deep and lasting effect on those who stay alive. It will be easier for our family and friends to remember us with joy and peace if we have said a grateful good-bye than if we die with bitter and disillusioned hearts.

The greatest gift we can offer our families and friends is the gift of gratitude. Gratitude sets them free to continue living without bitterness or self-recrimination.

The Companionship of the Dead

As we grow older we have more and more people to remember, people who have died before us. It is very important to remember those who have loved us and those we have loved. Remembering them means letting their spirits inspire us in our daily lives. They can become part of our spiritual communities and gently help us as we make decisions on our journeys. Parents, spouses, children, and friends can become true spiritual companions after they have died. Sometimes they can become even more intimate to us after death than when they were with us in life.

Remembering the dead is choosing their ongoing companionship.

Choosing Life

God says, "I am offering you life or death, blessing or curse. Choose life, then, so that you and your descendants may live" (Deuteronomy 30:19).

"Choose life." That's God's call for us, and there is not a moment in which we do not have to make that choice. Life and death are always before us. In our imaginations, our thoughts, our words, our gestures, our actions . . . even in our nonactions. This choice for life starts in a deep interior place. Underneath very life-affirming behavior I can still harbor death-thoughts and death-feelings. The most important question is not "Do I kill?" but "Do I carry a blessing in my heart or a curse?" The bullet that kills is only the final instrument of the hatred that began in the heart long before the gun was picked up.

❦

A Choice Calling for Discipline

When we look critically at the many thoughts and feelings that fill our minds and hearts, we may come to the horrifying discovery that we often choose death instead of life, curse instead of blessing. Jealousy, envy, anger, resentment, greed, lust, vindictiveness, revenge, hatred—they all float in that large reservoir of our inner life. Often we take them for granted and allow them to be there and do their destructive work.

But God asks us to choose life and to choose blessing. This choice requires an immense inner discipline. It requires a great attentiveness to the death-forces within us and a great commitment to let the forces of life come to dominate our thoughts and feelings. We cannot always do this alone; often we need a caring guide or a loving community to support us. But it is important that we both make the inner effort and seek the support we need from others to help us choose life.

SEPTEMBER

....

Claiming Our God-Given Selves

When we have been deeply hurt by another person, it is nearly impossible not to have hostile thoughts, feelings of anger or hatred, and even a desire to take revenge. All of this often happens spontaneously, without much inner control. We simply find ourselves brooding about what we are going to say or do to pay back the person who has hurt us. To choose blessings instead of curses in such a situation calls for an enormous leap of faith. It calls for a willingness to go beyond all our urges to get even and to choose a life-giving response.

Sometimes this seems impossible. Still, whenever we move beyond our wounded selves and claim our God-given selves, we give life not just to ourselves but also to the ones who have offended us.

Mastering Evil with Good

The apostle Paul writes to the Romans, "Bless your perse-
cutors; never curse them, bless them. . . . Never pay back
evil with evil. . . . Never try to get revenge. . . . If your
enemy is hungry, give him something to eat; if thirsty,
something to drink. . . . Do not be mastered by evil, but
master evil with good" (Romans 12:14–21). These words
cut to the heart of the spiritual life. They make it clear
what it means to choose life, not death, to choose blessings
not curses. But what is asked of us here goes against the
grain of our human nature. We will only be able to act according to Paul's words by knowing with our whole being
that what we are asked to do for others is what God has
done for us.

Waiting with Our Response

Choosing life instead of death demands an act of will that often contradicts our impulses. Our impulses want to take revenge, while our wills want to offer forgiveness. Our impulses push us to an immediate response: When someone hits us in the face, we impulsively want to hit back.

How then can we let our wills dominate our impulses? The key word is *wait*. Whatever happens, we must put some space between the hostile act directed toward us and our response. We must distance ourselves, take time to think, talk it over with friends, and wait until we are ready to respond in a life-giving way. Impulsive responses allow evil to master us, something we always will regret. But a well thought through response will help us to "master evil with good" (Romans 12:21).

Healing Letters

When you write a very angry letter to a friend who has hurt you deeply, don't send it! Let the letter sit on your table for a few days and read it over a number of times. Then ask yourself: "Will this letter bring life to me and my friend? Will it bring healing, will it bring a blessing?" You don't have to ignore the fact that you are deeply hurt. You don't have to hide from your friend that you feel offended. But you can respond in a way that makes healing and forgiveness possible and opens the door for new life. Rewrite the letter if you think it does not bring life, and send it with a prayer for your friend.

Choosing Words Wisely

Words are very important. When we say to someone, "You are an ugly, useless, despicable person," we might have ruined the possibility for a relationship with that person for life. Words can continue to do harm for many years.

It is so important to choose our words wisely. When we are boiling with anger and eager to throw bitter words at our opponents, it is better to remain silent. Words spoken in rage will make reconciliation very hard. Choosing life and not death, blessings and not curses, often starts by choosing to remain silent or choosing carefully the words that open the way to healing.

Speaking Words of Love

Often we remain silent when we need to speak. Without words, it is hard to love well. When we say to our parents, children, lovers, or friends, "I love you very much" or "I care for you" or "I think of you often" or "You are my greatest gift," we choose to give life.

It is not always easy to express our love directly in words. But whenever we do, we discover we have offered a blessing that will be long remembered. When a son can say to his father, "Dad, I love you," and when a mother can say to her daughter, "Child, I love you," a whole new blessed place can be opened up, a space where it is good to dwell. Indeed, words have the power to create life.

Blessing One Another

To bless means to say good things. We have to bless one another constantly. Parents need to bless their children, children their parents, husbands their wives, wives their husbands, friends their friends. In our society, so full of curses, we must fill each place we enter with our blessings. We forget so quickly that we are God's beloved children and allow the many curses of our world to darken our hearts. Therefore, we have to be reminded of our beloved-ness and remind others of theirs. Whether the blessing is given in words or with gestures, in a solemn or an informal way, our lives need to be blessed lives.

Choosing the Blessings

It is an ongoing temptation to think of ourselves as living under a curse. The loss of a friend, an illness, an accident, a natural disaster, a war, or any failure can make us quickly think that we are no good and are being punished. This temptation to think of our lives as full of curses is even greater when all the media present us day after day with stories about human misery.

Jesus came to bless us, not to curse us. But we must choose to receive that blessing and hand it on to others. Blessings and curses are always placed in front of us. We are free to choose. God says, Choose the blessings!

Living in the End-Time

We are living in the end-time! This does not mean that creation will soon come to its end, but it does mean that all the signs of the end of time that Jesus mentions are already with us: wars and revolutions, conflicts between nations and between kingdoms, earthquakes, plagues, famines, and persecutions (see Luke 21:9–12). Jesus describes the events of our world as announcements that this world is not our final dwelling place, but that the Son of Man will come to bring us our full freedom. "When these things begin to take place," Jesus says, "stand erect, hold your heads high, because your liberation is near at hand" (Luke 21:28). The terrible events surrounding us must be lived as ways to make us ready for our final liberation.

Opportunities to Witness

Jesus teaches us how to live in the present time. He identifies our present time as the end-time, the time that offers us countless opportunities to testify for Jesus and his Kingdom. The many disasters in our world, and all the tragedies that happen to people each day, can easily lead us to despair and convince us that we are the sad victims of circumstances. But Jesus looks at these events in a radically different way. He calls them opportunities to witness!

Jesus reminds us that we do not belong to this world. We have been sent into the world to be living witnesses of God's unconditional love, calling all people to look beyond the passing structures of our temporary existence to the eternal life promised to us.

Guarding Our Souls

The great danger of the turmoil of the end-time in which we live is losing our souls. Losing our souls means losing touch with our center, our true call in life, our mission, our spiritual task. Losing our souls means becoming so distracted by and preoccupied with all that is happening around us that we end up fragmented, confused, and erratic. Jesus is very aware of that danger. He says, "Take care not to be deceived, because many will come using my name and saying, 'I am the one' and 'The time is near at hand.' Refuse to join them" (Luke 21:8).

In the midst of anxious times there are many false prophets, promising all sorts of "salvations." It is important that we be faithful disciples of Jesus, never losing touch with our true spiritual selves.

Holding Our Ground

In a world so full of social and political turmoil and immense human suffering, people of faith will often be ridiculed because of their so-called ineffectiveness. Many will say, "If you believe that there is a loving God, let your God do something about this mess!" Some will simply declare religion irrelevant, while others will consider it an obstacle to the creation of a new and better world.

Jesus often tells his followers that, as he was, they will be persecuted, arrested, tortured, and killed. But he also tells us not to worry but to trust in him at all times. "Make up your minds not to prepare your defense, because I myself shall give you an eloquence and a wisdom that none of your opponents will be able to resist or contradict" (Luke 21:14–15). Let's not be afraid of skepticism and cynicism coming our way, but trust that God will give us the strength to hold our ground.

Remaining Anchored in Love

When we are anxious we are inclined to overprepare. We wonder what to say when we are attacked, how to respond when we are being interrogated, and what defense to put up when we are accused. It is precisely this turmoil that makes us lose our self-confidence and creates in us a debilitating self-consciousness.

Jesus tells us not to worry at all and to trust that he will give us the words and wisdom we need. What is important is not that we have a little speech ready but that we remain deeply anchored in the love of Jesus, secure about who we are in this world and why we are here. With our hearts connected to the heart of Jesus, we will always know what to say when the time to speak comes.

Remaining Faithful

Many people live with the unconscious or conscious expectation that eventually things will get better; wars, hunger, poverty, oppression, and exploitation will vanish; and all people will live in harmony. Their lives and work are motivated by that expectation. When this does not happen in their lifetimes, they are often disillusioned and experience themselves as failures.

But Jesus doesn't support such an optimistic outlook. He foresees not only the destruction of his beloved city Jerusalem but also a world full of cruelty, violence, and conflict. For Jesus there is no happy ending in this world. The challenge of Jesus is not to solve all the world's problems before the end of time but to remain faithful at any cost.

Keeping It Together

How can we not lose our souls when everything and every-body pulls us in different directions? How can we "keep it together" when we are constantly being torn apart?

Jesus says, "Not a hair of your head will be lost. Your perseverance will win you your lives" (Luke 21:18–19). We can only survive our world when we trust that God knows us more intimately than we know ourselves. We can only keep it together when we believe that God holds us together. We can only win our lives when we remain faithful to the truth that every little part of us, yes, every hair, is completely safe in the divine embrace of our Lord. To say it differently: When we keep living a spiritual life, we have nothing to be afraid of.

The Coming of the Son of Man

The spiritual knowledge that we belong to God and are safe with God even as we live in a very destructive world allows us to see in the midst of all the turmoil, fear, and agony of history "the Son of Man coming in a cloud with power and great glory" (Luke 21:27). Even though Jesus speaks about this as about a final event, it is not just one more thing that is going to happen after all the terrible things are over. Just as the end-time is already here, so too is the coming of the Son of Man. It is an event in the realm of the Spirit and thus not subject to the boundaries of time.

Those who live in communion with Jesus have the eyes to see and the ears to hear the second coming of Jesus among them in the here and now. Jesus says, "Before this generation has passed away all will have taken place" (Luke 21:32). And this is true for each faithful generation.

Standing Erect

About the end-time Jesus says, "There will be signs in the sun and moon and stars; on earth nations in agony, bewildered by the turmoil of the ocean and its waves; men fainting away with terror and fear at what menaces the world, for the power of heaven will be shaken. And then they will see the Son of Man coming in a cloud with power and great glory" (Luke 21:25–28). All of this is already taking place. For anyone who has listened deeply to the heart of God, the despair of the world and the coming of the great liberation are both visible every day.

What then should we do? Jesus says it clearly, "Stand erect, hold your heads high, because your liberation is near at hand" (Luke 21:28). There is so much hope here. We do not have to faint but can stand straight, welcoming our Lord with outstretched arms.

Living in a State of Preparedness

Everything that comes from God asks for an open and faithful heart. We cannot live with hope and joy in the end-time unless we are living in a state of preparedness. We have to be careful because, as the apostle Peter says, "Your enemy the devil is on the prowl like a roaring lion, looking for someone to devour" (1 Peter 5:8). Therefore, Jesus says, "Watch yourselves, or your hearts will be coarsened by debauchery and drunkenness and the cares of life. . . . Stay awake, praying at all times for the strength to survive all that is going to happen, and to hold your ground before the Son of Man" (Luke 21:34–36). That's what living in the Spirit of Jesus calls us to.

Standing Under the Cross

Standing erect, holding our heads high, is the attitude of spiritually mature people in face of the calamities of our world. The facts of everyday life are a rich source for doomsday thinking and feeling. But it is possible for us to resist this temptation and to stand with self-confidence in this world, never losing our spiritual ground, always aware that "sky and earth will pass away" but the words of Jesus will never pass away (see Luke 21:33).

Let us be like Mary, the mother of Jesus, who *stood* under the cross, trusting in God's faithfulness notwithstanding the death of his beloved Child.

Keeping Close to the Word of Jesus

The words of Jesus can keep us erect and confident in the midst of the turmoil of the end-time. They can support us, encourage us, and give us life even when everything around us speaks of death. Jesus' words are food for eternal life. They do much more than give us ideas and inspiration. They lead us into the eternal life while we are still being clothed in mortal flesh.

When we keep close to the word of Jesus, reflecting on it, "chewing" on it, eating it as food for the soul, we will enter even more deeply into the everlasting love of God.

Meditation

When Jesus says, "Sky and earth will pass away, but my words will never pass away" (Luke 21:33), he shows us a direct way to eternal life. The words of Jesus have the power to transform our hearts and minds and lead us into the Kingdom of God. "The words I have spoken to you," Jesus says, "are spirit and they are life" (John 6:63).

Through meditation we can let the words of Jesus descend from our minds into our hearts and create there a dwelling place for the Spirit. Whatever we do and wherever we go, let us stay close to the words of Jesus. They are words of eternal life.

The Created Order as Sacrament

When God took on flesh in Jesus Christ, the uncreated and the created, the eternal and the temporal, the divine and the human, became united. This unity meant that all that is mortal now points to the immortal, all that is finite now points to the infinite. In and through Jesus all creation has become like a splendid veil, through which the face of God is revealed to us.

This is called the sacramental quality of the created order. All that is is sacred because all that is speaks of God's redeeming love. Seas and winds, mountains and trees, sun, moon, and stars, and all the animals and people have become sacred windows offering us glimpses of God.

The Sacredness of God's Handiwork

How do we live in creation? Do we relate to it as a place full of "things" we can use for whatever need we want to fulfill and whatever goal we wish to accomplish? Or do we see creation first of all as a sacramental reality, a sacred space where God reveals to us the immense beauty of the Divine?

As long as we only *use* creation, we cannot recognize its sacredness because we are approaching it as if we were its owners. But when we relate to all that surrounds us as created by the same God who created us and as the place where God appears to us and calls us to worship and adoration, then we are able to recognize the sacredness of all God's handiwork.

Baptism and Eucharist

Sacraments are very specific events in which God touches us through creation and transforms us into living Christs. The two main sacraments are baptism and the Eucharist. In baptism water is the way to transformation. In the Eucharist it is bread and wine. The most ordinary things in life—water, bread, and wine—become the sacred way by which God comes to us.

These sacraments are actual events. Water, bread, and wine are not simply reminders of God's love; they bring God to us. In baptism we are set free from the slavery of sin and dressed with Christ. In the Eucharist, Christ himself becomes our food and drink.

Baptism, Becoming Children of the Light

When Jesus appears for the last time to his disciples, he sends them out into the world saying, "Go . . . make disciples of all nations; baptize them in the name of the Father and of the Son and of the Holy Spirit" (Matthew 28:19).

Jesus offers us baptism as the way to enter into communion with God, Father, Son, and Spirit, and to live our lives as God's beloved children. Through baptism we say no to the world. We declare that we no longer want to remain children of the darkness but want to become children of the light, God's children. We do not want to escape the world, but we want to live in it without belonging to it. That is what baptism enables us to do.

Baptism, a Rite of Passage

Baptism is a rite of passage. The Jewish people passed through the Red Sea to the Promised Land in the great exodus. Jesus himself wanted to make this exodus by passing through suffering and death into the house of his heavenly Father. This was his baptism. He asked his disciples and now asks us, "Can you ... be baptised with the baptism with which I shall be baptised?" (Mark 10:38). When the apostle Paul, therefore, speaks about our baptism, he calls it a baptism into Jesus' death (Romans 6:4).

To be baptized means to make the passage with the people of Israel and with Jesus from slavery to freedom and from death to new life. It is a commitment to a life in and through Jesus.

Baptism, the Way to Freedom

When parents have their children baptized they indicate their desire to have their children grow up and live as children of God and brothers or sisters of Jesus, and be guided by the Holy Spirit.

Through birth a child is given to parents; through baptism a child is given to God. At baptism the parents acknowledge that their parenthood is a participation in God's parenthood, that all fatherhood and motherhood comes from God. Thus, baptism frees the parents from a sense of owning their children. Children belong to God and are given to the parents to love and care for in God's name. It is the parents' vocation to welcome their children as honored guests in their home and bring them to the physical, emotional, and spiritual freedom that enables them to leave the home and become parents themselves. Baptism reminds parents of this vocation and sets children on the path of freedom.

❧

Baptism, the Way to Community

Baptism is more than a way to spiritual freedom. It is also the way to community. Baptizing a person, whether child or adult, is receiving that person into the community of faith. Those who are reborn from above through baptism, and are called to live the life of sons and daughters of God, belong together as members of one spiritual family, the living body of Christ. When we baptize people, we welcome them into this family of God and offer them guidance, support, and formation as they grow to the full maturity of the Christ-like life.

Baptism, a Call to Commitment

Baptism as a way to the freedom of the children of God and as a way to a life in community calls for a personal commitment. There is nothing magical or automatic about this sacrament. Having water poured over us while someone says, "I baptize you in the Name of the Father and the Son and the Holy Spirit," has lasting significance only when we are willing to claim and reclaim in all possible ways the spiritual truth of who we are as baptized people.

In this sense baptism is a call to parents of baptized children and to the baptized themselves to choose constantly for the light in the midst of a dark world and for life in the midst of a death-harboring society.

Eucharist, the Sacrament of Communion

Baptism opens the door to the Eucharist. The Eucharist is the sacrament through which Jesus enters into an intimate, permanent communion with us. It is the sacrament of the table. It is the sacrament of food and drink. It is the sacrament of daily nurture. While baptism is a once-in-a-lifetime event, the Eucharist can be a monthly, weekly, or even daily occurrence. Jesus gave us the Eucharist in memory of his life and death. Not a memory that simply makes us think of him but a memory that makes us members of his body. That is why Jesus on the evening before he died took bread, saying, "This is my Body," and took the cup, saying, "This is my Blood." By eating the Body and drinking the Blood of Christ, we become one with him.

OCTOBER

❦

. . . .

Jesus Gives Himself to Us

When we invite friends for a meal, we do much more than offer them food for their bodies. We offer friendship, fellowship, good conversation, intimacy, and closeness. When we say, "Help yourself . . . take some more . . . don't be shy . . . have another glass," we offer our guests not only our food and our drink but also ourselves. A spiritual bond grows, and we become food and drink for one another.

In the most complete and perfect way, this happens when Jesus gives himself to us in the Eucharist as food and drink. By offering us his Body and Blood, Jesus offers us the most intimate communion possible. It is a divine communion.

The Most Human and Most Divine Gesture

The two disciples whom Jesus joined on the road to Emmaus recognized him in the breaking of the bread. What is a more common, ordinary gesture than breaking bread? It may be the most human of all human gestures: a gesture of hospitality, friendship, care, and the desire to be together. Taking a loaf of bread, blessing it, breaking it, and giving it to those seated around the table signifies unity, community, and peace. When Jesus does this he does the most ordinary as well as the most extraordinary. It is the most human as well as the most divine gesture.

The great mystery is that this daily and most human gesture is the way we recognize the presence of Christ among us. God becomes most present when we are most human.

❧

A Place of Vulnerability and Trust

When we gather around the table and eat from the same loaf and drink from the same cup, we are most vulnerable to one another. We cannot have a meal together in peace with guns hanging over our shoulders and pistols attached to our belts. When we break bread together we leave our arms—whether they are physical or mental—at the door and enter into a place of mutual vulnerability and trust.

The beauty of the Eucharist is precisely that it is the place where a vulnerable God invites vulnerable people to come together in a peaceful meal. When we break bread and give it to each other, fear vanishes and God becomes very close.

Jesus, Our Food and Drink

Jesus is the Word of God, who came down from heaven, was born of the Virgin Mary through the power of the Holy Spirit, and became a human being. This happened in a specific place at a specific time. But each day when we celebrate the Eucharist, Jesus comes down from heaven, takes bread and wine, and by the power of the Holy Spirit becomes our food and drink. Indeed, through the Eucharist, God's incarnation continues to happen at any time and at any place.

Sometimes we might think, "I wish I had been there with Jesus and his apostles long ago!" But Jesus is closer to us now than he was to his own friends. Today he is our daily bread!

The Companion of Our Souls

When the two disciples recognized Jesus as he broke the bread for them in their house in Emmaus, he "vanished from their sight" (Luke 24:31). The recognition and the disappearance of Jesus are one and the same event. Why? Because the disciples recognized that their Lord Jesus, the Christ, now lives in them . . . that they have become Christ-bearers. Therefore, Jesus no longer sits across the table from them as the stranger, the guest, the friend with whom they can speak and from whom they can receive good counsel. He has become one with them. He has given them his own Spirit of Love. Their companion on the journey has become the companion of their souls. They are alive, yet it is no longer them, but Christ living in them (see Galatians 2:20).

Jesus Living Within Us

When we gather around the Eucharistic table and eat from the same bread and drink from the same cup, saying, "This is the Body and Blood of Christ," we become the living Christ, here and now.

Our faith in Jesus is not our belief that Jesus, the Son of God, lived long ago, performed great miracles, presented wise teachings, died for us on the cross, and rose from the grave. It first of all means that we fully accept the truth that Jesus lives within us and fulfills his divine ministry in and through us. This spiritual knowledge of the Christ living in us is what allows us to affirm fully the mystery of the incarnation, death, and resurrection as historic events. It is the Christ in us who reveals to us the Christ in history.

Jesus Living Among Us

The Eucharist is the place where Jesus becomes most present to us because he becomes not only the Christ living within us but also the Christ living among us. Just as the disciples at Emmaus who had recognized Jesus in the breaking of the bread discovered a new intimacy between themselves and found the courage to return to their friends, we who have received the Body and Blood of Jesus will find a new unity among ourselves. As we realize that Christ lives within us, we also come to realize that Christ lives among us and makes us into a body of people witnessing together to the presence of Christ in the world.

The Sacrament of Unity

The Eucharist is the sacrament of unity. It makes us into one body. The apostle Paul writes, "As there is one loaf, so we, although there are many of us, are one single body, for we all share in the one loaf" (1 Corinthians 10:17).

The Eucharist is much more than a place where we celebrate our unity in Christ. The Eucharist creates this unity. By eating from the same bread and drinking from the same cup, we become the body of Christ present in the world. Just as Christ becomes really present to us in the breaking of the bread, we become really present to one another as brothers and sisters of Christ, members of the same body. Thus, the Eucharist not only signifies unity but also creates it.

Christ's Body, Our Body

When we gather for the Eucharist we gather in the Name of Jesus, who is calling us together to remember his death and resurrection in the breaking of the bread. There he is truly among us. "Where two or three meet in my name," he says, "I am there among them" (Matthew 18:20).

The presence of Jesus among us and in the gifts of bread and wine are the same presence. As we recognize Jesus in the breaking of the bread, we recognize him also in our brothers and sisters. As we give one another the bread, saying, "This is the Body of Christ," we give ourselves to one another, saying, "We are the Body of Christ." It is one and the same giving, it is one and the same body, it is one and the same Christ.

Breaking Through
the Boundaries

The sacrament of the Eucharist, as the sacrament of the presence of Christ among and within us, has the unique power to unite us into one body, irrespective of age, color, race or gender, emotional condition, economic status, or social background. The Eucharist breaks through all these boundaries and creates the one body of Christ, living in the world as a vibrant sign of unity and community.

Jesus prays fervently to his Father, "May they all be one, just as, Father, you are in me and I am in you, so that they also may be in us, so that the world may believe it was you who sent me" (John 17:21). The Eucharist is the sacrament of this divine unity lived out among all people.

৽৳৵

Knowing One Another in Christ

Often we think that we first have to know and understand one another before we gather around the Eucharistic table. Although it is good if those who share in the Body and Blood of Christ know one another personally, coming together regularly for the Eucharist creates a spiritual unity that goes far beyond the various levels of "knowing one another" in human ways. As we enter together into the sacred mysteries of the death and resurrection of Jesus by participating in the Eucharist, we gradually become one body. We truly come to know one another *in* Christ.

Deepening the Passage of Baptism

In and through the celebration of the Eucharist, Jesus' death and resurrection become a reality for us here and now. As we eat and drink from the Body and Blood of Christ, our mortal bodies become united with the risen Christ. Thus, our deaths, like Jesus' death, mean not destruction but passage to new life.

In this way the Eucharist deepens and strengthens in us the passage that we first made through baptism. The Eucharist is the sacrament that allows us to appropriate fully our baptismal grace.

❧

Becoming the Mystical Body of Christ

As we gather around the Eucharistic table and make the death and resurrection of Jesus our own by sharing in the "bread of life" and the "cup of salvation," we become together the living body of Christ.

The Eucharist is the sacrament by which we become one body. Becoming one body is not becoming a team or a group or even a fellowship. Becoming one body is becoming the body of Christ. It is becoming the living Lord, visibly present in the world. It is—as often has been said—becoming the mystical Body of Christ. But *mystical* and *real* are the same in the realm of the Spirit.

Really Present

Where is Jesus today? Jesus is where those who believe in him and express that belief in baptism and the Eucharist become one body. As long as we think about the body of believers as a group of people who share a common faith in Jesus of Nazareth, Jesus remains an inspirational historical figure. But when we realize that the body Jesus fashions in the Eucharist is *his* body, we can start to see what real presence is. Jesus, who is present in the gifts of his Body and Blood, becomes present in the body of believers that is formed by these gifts. We who receive the Body of Christ become the living Christ.

The Pillars of the Church

The two main sacraments, baptism and the Eucharist, are the spiritual pillars of the Church. They are not simply instruments by which the Church exercises its ministry. They are not just means by which we become and remain members of the Church but belong to the essence of the Church. Without these sacraments there is no Church. The Church is the body of Christ fashioned by baptism and the Eucharist. When people are baptized in the Name of the Father and the Son and the Holy Spirit, and when they gather around the table of Christ and receive his Body and Blood, they become the people of God, called the Church.

Called out of Slavery

The Church is the people of God. The Latin word for "church," *ecclesia,* comes from the Greek *ek,* which means "out," and *kaleo,* which means "to call." The Church is the people of God called out of slavery to freedom, sin to salvation, despair to hope, darkness to light, an existence centered on death to an existence focused on life.

When we think of the Church we have to think of a body of people, traveling together. We have to envision women, men, and children of all ages, races, and societies supporting one another on their long and often tiresome journeys to their final home.

The Church, Spotless and Tainted

The Church is holy *and* sinful, spotless *and* tainted. The Church is the bride of Christ, who washed her in cleansing water and took her to himself "with no speck or wrinkle or anything like that, but holy and faultless" (Ephesians 5:26–27). The Church too is a group of sinful, confused, anguished people constantly tempted by the powers of lust and greed and always entangled in rivalry and competition.

When we say that the Church is a body, we refer not only to the holy and faultless body made Christ-like through baptism and Eucharist but also to the broken bodies of all the people who are its members. Only when we keep both these ways of thinking and speaking together can we live in the Church as true followers of Jesus.

Believing in the Church

The Church is an object of faith. In the Apostles' Creed we pray, "I believe in God, the Father, . . . in Jesus Christ, his only Son . . . in the Holy Spirit, the holy catholic Church, the communion of saints, the forgiveness of sins, the resurrection of the body and the life everlasting." We must believe in the Church! The Apostles' Creed does not say that the Church is an organization that helps us to believe in God, Father, Son, and Holy Spirit. No, we are called to believe in the Church with the same faith we believe in God.

Often it seems harder to believe in the Church than to believe in God. But whenever we separate our belief in God from our belief in the Church, we become unbelievers. God has given us the Church as the place where God becomes God-with-us.

The Two Sides of One Faith

Our faith in God who sent his Son to become God-with-us and who, with his Son, sent his Spirit to become God-within-us cannot be real without our faith in the Church. The Church is that unlikely body of people through whom God chooses to reveal God's love for us. Just as it seems unlikely to us that God chose to become human in a young girl living in a small, not very respected town in the Middle East nearly two thousand years ago, it seems unlikely that God chose to continue his work of salvation in a community of people constantly torn apart by arguments, prejudices, authority conflicts, and power games.

Still, believing in Jesus and believing in the Church are two sides of one faith. It is unlikely but divine!

Superabundant Grace

Over the centuries the Church has done enough to make any critical person want to leave it. Its history of violent crusades, pogroms, power struggles, oppression, excommunications, executions, manipulation of people and ideas, and constantly recurring divisions is there for everyone to see and be appalled by.

Can we believe that this is the same Church that carries in its center the Word of God and the sacraments of God's healing love? Can we trust that in the midst of all its human brokenness the Church presents the broken body of Christ to the world as food for eternal life? Can we acknowledge that where sin is abundant grace is superabundant, and that where promises are broken over and over again God's promise stands unshaken? To believe is to answer yes to these questions.

The Church, God's People

As Jesus was one human person among many, the Church is one organization among many. And just as there may have been people with more attractive appearances than Jesus, there may be many organizations that are a lot better run than the Church. But Jesus is the Christ appearing among us to reveal God's love, and the Church is his people called together to make his presence visible in today's world.

Would we have recognized Jesus as the Christ if we had met him many years ago? Are we able to recognize him today in his body, the Church? We are asked to make a leap of faith. If we dare to do it our eyes will be opened and we will see the glory of God.

The Garden of the Saints

The Church is a very human organization but also the garden of God's grace. It is a place where great sanctity keeps blooming. Saints are people who make the living Christ visible to us in a special way. Some saints have given their lives in the service of Christ and his Church; others have spoken and written words that keep nurturing us; some have lived heroically in difficult situations; others have remained hidden in quiet lives of prayer and meditation; some were prophetic voices calling for renewal; others were spiritual strategists setting up large organizations or networks of people; some were healthy and strong; others were quite sick, and often anxious and insecure.

But all of them in their own ways lived in the Church as in a garden where they heard the voice calling them the Beloved and where they found the courage to make Jesus the center of their lives.

Being *in* the Church, Not *of* It

Often we hear the remark that we have to live *in* the world without being *of* the world. But it may be more difficult to be *in* the Church without being *of* the Church. Being *of* the Church means being so preoccupied by and involved in the many ecclesial affairs and clerical "ins and outs" that we are no longer focused on Jesus. The Church then blinds us to what we came to see and deafens us to what we came to hear. Still, it is *in* the Church that Christ dwells, invites us to his table, and speaks to us words of eternal love.

Being *in* the Church without being *of* it is a great spiritual challenge.

Loving the Church

Loving the Church often seems close to impossible. Still, we must keep reminding ourselves that all people in the Church—whether powerful or powerless, conservative or progressive, tolerant or fanatic—belong to that long line of witnesses moving through this valley of tears, singing songs of praise and thanksgiving, listening to the voice of their Lord, and eating together from the bread that keeps multiplying as it is shared. When we remember that, we may be able to say, "I love the Church, and I am glad to belong to it."

Loving the Church is our sacred duty. Without a true love for the Church, we cannot live in it in joy and peace. And without a true love for the Church, we cannot call people to it.

Meeting Christ in the Church

Loving the Church does not require romantic emotions. It requires the will to see the living Christ among his people and to love them as we want to love Christ himself. This is true not only for the "little" people—the poor, the oppressed, the forgotten—but also for the "big" people who exercise authority in the Church.

To love the Church means to be willing to meet Jesus wherever we go in the Church. This love doesn't mean agreeing with or approving of everyone's ideas or behavior. On the contrary, it can call us to confront those who hide Christ from us. But whether we confront or affirm, criticize or praise, we can only become fruitful when our words and actions come from hearts that love the Church.

The Authority of Compassion

The Church often wounds us deeply. People with religious authority often wound us by their words, attitudes, and demands. Precisely because our religion brings us in touch with the questions of life and death, our religious sensibilities can get hurt most easily. Ministers and priests seldom fully realize how a critical remark, a gesture of rejection, or an act of impatience can be remembered for life by those to whom it is directed.

There is such an enormous hunger for meaning in life, for comfort and consolation, for forgiveness and reconciliation, for restoration and healing, that anyone who has any authority in the Church should constantly be reminded that the best word to characterize religious authority is *compassion*. Let's keep looking at Jesus, whose authority was expressed in compassion.

Forgiving the Church

When we have been wounded by the Church, our temptation is to reject it. But when we reject the Church it becomes very hard for us to keep in touch with the living Christ. When we say, "I love Jesus, but I hate the Church," we end up losing not only the Church but Jesus too. The challenge is to forgive the Church. This challenge is especially great because the Church seldom asks us for forgiveness, at least not officially. But the Church as an often fallible human organization needs our forgiveness, while the Church as the living Christ among us continues to offer us forgiveness.

It is important to think about the Church not as "over there" but as a community of struggling, weak people of whom we are part and in whom we meet our Lord and Redeemer.

Our Spiritual Leaders

The Church as the body of Christ has many faces. The Church prays and worships. It speaks words of instruction and healing, cleanses us from our sins, invites us to the table of the Lord, binds us together in a covenant of love, sends us out to minister, anoints us when we are sick or dying, and accompanies us in our search for meaning and our daily need for support. All these faces might not come to us from those we look up to as our leaders. But when we live our lives with a simple trust that Jesus comes to us in our Church, we will see the Church's ministry in places and in faces where we least expect it.

If we truly love Jesus, Jesus will send us the people to give us what we most need. And they *are* our spiritual leaders.

One Body with Many Parts

The Church is one body. Paul writes, "We were baptised into one body in a single Spirit" (1 Corinthians 12:13). But this one body has many parts. As Paul says, "If they were all the same part, how could it be a body? As it is, the parts are many but the body is one" (1 Corinthians 12:19). Not everyone can be everything. Often we expect one member of the body to fulfill a task that belongs to others. But the hand cannot be asked to see nor the eye to hear.

Together we are Christ's body, each of us with a part to play in the whole (see 1 Corinthians 12:27). Let's be grateful for our limited but real part in the body.

The Weakest in the Center

The most honored parts of the body are not the head or the hands, which lead and control. The most important parts are the least presentable parts. That's the mystery of the Church. As a people called out of oppression to freedom, we must recognize that it is the weakest among us—the elderly, the small children, the handicapped, the mentally ill, the hungry and sick—who form the real center. Paul says, "It is the parts of the body which we consider least dignified that we surround with the greatest dignity" (1 Corinthians 12:23).

The Church as the people of God can truly embody the living Christ among us only when the poor remain its most treasured part. Care for the poor, therefore, is much more than Christian charity. It is the essence of being the body of Christ.

Focusing on the Poor

Like every human organization the Church is constantly in danger of corruption. As soon as power and wealth come to the Church, manipulation, exploitation, misuse of influence, and outright corruption are not far away.

How do we prevent corruption in the Church? The answer is clear: by focusing on the poor. The poor make the Church faithful to its vocation. When the Church is no longer a church for the poor, it loses its spiritual identity. It gets caught up in disagreements, jealousy, power games, and pettiness. Paul says, "God has composed the body so that greater dignity is given to the parts which were without it, and so that there may not be disagreements inside the body but each part may be equally concerned for all the others" (1 Corinthians 12:24–25). This is the true vision. The poor are given to the Church so that the Church as the body of Christ can be and remain a place of mutual concern, love, and peace.

NOVEMBER

❧

· ·

Going to the Margins of the Church

Those who are marginal in the world are central in the Church, and that is how it is supposed to be! Thus we are called as members of the Church to keep going to the margins of our society. The homeless, the starving, parentless children, people with AIDS, our emotionally disturbed brothers and sisters—they require our first attention.

We can trust that when we reach out with all our energy to the margins of our society we will discover that petty disagreements, fruitless debates, and paralyzing rivalries will recede and gradually vanish. The Church will always be renewed when our attention shifts from ourselves to those who need our care. The blessing of Jesus always comes to us through the poor. The most remarkable experience of those who work with the poor is that, in the end, the poor give more than they receive. They give food to us.

Who Are the Poor?

The poor are the center of the Church. But who are the poor? At first we might think of people who are not like us: people who live in slums, people who go to soup kitchens, people who sleep on the streets, people in prisons, mental hospitals, and nursing homes. But the poor can be very close. They can be in our own families, churches, or workplaces. Even closer, the poor can be ourselves, who feel unloved, rejected, ignored, or abused.

It is precisely when we see and experience poverty—whether far away, close by, or in our own hearts—that we need to become the Church; that is, hold hands as brothers and sisters, confess our own brokenness and need, forgive one another, heal one another's wounds, and gather around the table of Jesus for the breaking of the bread. Thus, as the poor *we* recognize Jesus, who became poor for us.

Becoming the Church
of the Poor

When we claim our own poverty and connect our poverty with the poverty of our brothers and sisters, we become the Church of the poor, which is the Church of Jesus. Solidarity is essential for the Church of the poor. Both pain and joy must be shared. As one body we experience deeply one another's agonies as well as one another's ecstasies. As Paul says, "If one part is hurt, all the parts share its pain. And if one part is honored, all the parts share its joy" (1 Corinthians 12:26).

Often we might prefer not to be part of the body because this participation makes us feel the pain of others so intensely. Every time we love others deeply we feel their pain deeply. However, joy is hidden in the pain. When we share the pain we will also share the joy.

❦

The Poverty of Our Leaders

There is a tendency to think about poverty, suffering, and pain as realities that happen primarily or even exclusively at the bottom of our Church. We seldom think of our leaders as poor. Still, there is great poverty, deep loneliness, painful isolation, real depression, and much emotional suffering at the top of our Church.

We need the courage to acknowledge the suffering of the leaders of our Church—its ministers, priests, bishops, and popes—and include them in this fellowship of the weak. When we are not distracted by the power, wealth, and success of those who offer leadership, we will soon discover their powerlessness, poverty, and failures and feel free to reach out to them with the same compassion we want to give to those at the bottom. In God's eyes there is no distance between bottom and top. There shouldn't be in our eyes either.

❦

The Mission of the Church

There are more people on this planet outside the Church than inside it. Millions have been baptized, millions have not. Millions participate in the celebration of the Lord's Supper, but millions do not.

The Church as the body of Christ, as Christ living in the world, has a larger mission than to support, nurture, and guide its own members. It is also called to be a witness to the love of God made visible in Jesus. Before his death Jesus prayed for his followers, "As you sent me into the world, I have sent them into the world" (John 17:18). Part of the essence of being the Church is being a living witness for Christ in the world.

☙❧

A Ministry of Healing and Reconciliation

How does the Church witness to Christ in the world? First and foremost by giving visibility to Jesus' love for the poor and the weak. In a world so hungry for healing, forgiveness, reconciliation, and most of all unconditional love, the Church must alleviate that hunger through its ministry. Wherever we feed the hungry, clothe the naked, visit the lonely, listen to those who are rejected, and bring unity and peace to those who are divided, we proclaim the living Christ, whether we speak about him or not.

It is important that whatever we do and wherever we go, we remain in the Name of Jesus, who sent us. Outside his Name our ministry will lose its divine energy.

Telling the Story of Jesus

The Church is called to announce the Good News of Jesus to all people and all nations. Besides the many works of mercy by which the Church must make Jesus' love visible, it must also joyfully announce the great mystery of God's salvation through the life, suffering, death, and resurrection of Jesus. The story of Jesus is to be proclaimed and celebrated. Some will hear and rejoice, some will remain indifferent, some will become hostile. The story of Jesus will not always be accepted, but it must be told.

We who know the story and try to live it out have the joyful task of telling it to others. When our words rise from hearts full of love and gratitude, they will bear fruit, whether we can see this or not.

❧

The Communion of Saints

We often limit the Church to the organization of people who identify themselves clearly as its members. But the Church as all people belonging to Christ, as that body of witnesses who reveal the living Christ, reaches far beyond the boundaries of any human institution. As Jesus himself said, The Spirit "blows where it pleases" (John 3:8). The Spirit of Jesus can touch hearts wherever it wants; it is not restrained by any human limits.

There is a communion of saints witnessing to the risen Christ that reaches to the far ends of the world and even farther. It embraces people from long ago and far away. It is that immense community of men and women who through words and deeds have proclaimed and are proclaiming the Lordship of Jesus.

The Saints Who Live Short Lives

As we see so many people die at a young age, through wars, starvation, AIDS, street violence, and physical and emotional neglect, we often wonder what the value of their short lives is. It seems that their journeys have been cut off before they could reach any of their goals, realize any of their dreams, or accomplish any of their tasks. But, short as their lives may have been, they belong to that immense communion of saints, from all times and all places, who stand around the throne of the Lamb dressed in white robes proclaiming the victory of the crucified Christ (see Revelation 7:9).

The story of the innocent children murdered by King Herod in his attempt to destroy Jesus (see Matthew 2:13–18), reminds us that saintliness is not just for those who lived long and hardworking lives. These children, and many others who died young, are as much witnesses to Jesus as those who accomplished heroic deeds.

Saints, People Like Us

Through baptism we become part of a family much larger than our biological family. It is a family of people "set apart" by God to be light in the darkness. These set-apart people are called saints. Although we tend to think about saints as holy and pious, and picture them with halos above their heads and ecstatic gazes, true saints are much more accessible. They are men and women like us, who live ordinary lives and struggle with ordinary problems. What makes them saints is their clear and unwavering focus on God and God's people. Some of their lives may look quite different, but most of their lives are remarkably similar to our own.

The saints are our brothers and sisters, calling us to become like them.

The Large Network of God's People

The saints are God's holy people. The apostle Paul speaks about all those who belong to Christ as "holy people" or "saints." He directs his letters to "those who have been consecrated in Christ Jesus and called to be God's holy people" (1 Corinthians 1:2; see also Ephesians 1:1). This sanctity is the work of the Spirit of Jesus. Paul again says, "All of us, with our unveiled faces like mirrors reflecting the glory of the Lord, are being transformed into the image that we reflect in brighter and brighter glory; this is the working of the Lord who is the Spirit" (2 Corinthians 3:18).

As saints we belong to that large network of God's people that shines like a multitude of stars in the dark sky of the universe.

❧

In Memory of Jesus and the Saints

Belonging to the communion of saints means being connected with all people transformed by the Spirit of Jesus. This connection is deep and intimate. Those who have lived as brothers and sisters of Jesus continue to live within us, even though they have died, just as Jesus continues to live within us, even though *he* has died.

We live our lives in memory of Jesus and the saints, and this memory is a real presence. Jesus and his saints are part of our most intimate and spiritual knowledge of God. They inspire us, guide us, encourage us, and give us hope. They are the source of our constant transformation. Yes, we carry them in our hearts and thus keep them alive for all with whom we live and work.

Hearts As Wide As the World

The awareness of being part of the communion of saints makes our hearts as wide as the world. The love with which we love is not just our love; it is the love of Jesus and his saints living in us. When the Spirit of Jesus lives in our hearts, all who have lived their lives in that Spirit live there too. Our parents, grandparents, and great-grandparents; our teachers and their teachers; our pastors and their pastors; our spiritual guides and theirs—all the holy men and women who form that long line of love through history—are part of our hearts, where the Spirit of Jesus chooses to dwell.

The communion of saints is not just a network of connections between people. It is first and foremost the community of our hearts.

The Fruit of Our Communal Life

Our society encourages individualism. We are constantly made to believe that everything we think, say, or do is our personal accomplishment, deserving individual attention. But as people who belong to the communion of saints, we know that anything of spiritual value is not the result of individual accomplishment but the fruit of a communal life.

Whatever we know about God and God's love, whatever we know about Jesus—his life, death, and resurrection—whatever we know about the Church and its ministry, is not the invention of our minds asking for an award. It is the knowledge that has come to us through the ages from the people of Israel and the prophets, from Jesus and the saints, and from all who have played roles in the formation of our hearts. True spiritual knowledge belongs to the communion of saints.

❧

Embracing the Universe

Living a spiritual life makes our little, fearful hearts as wide as the universe, because the Spirit of Jesus dwelling within us embraces the whole of creation. Jesus is the Word, through whom the universe has been created. As Paul says, "In him were created all things in heaven and on earth: everything visible and everything invisible—all things were created through him and for him—in him all things hold together" (Collossians 1:16–17). Therefore, when Jesus lives within us through his Spirit, our hearts embrace not only all people but all of creation. Love casts out all fear and gathers in all that belongs to God.

Prayer, which is breathing with the Spirit of Jesus, leads us to this immense knowledge.

Unity in the Heart of God

Love unites all, whether created or uncreated. The heart of
God, the heart of all creation, and our own hearts become
one in love. That's what all the great mystics have been trying to tell us through the ages. Benedict, Francis, Hildegard
of Bingen, Hadewijch of Brabant, Meister Eckhart, Teresa
of Avila, John of the Cross, Dag Hammarskjöld, Thomas
Merton, and many others, all in their own ways and their
own languages, have witnessed to the unifying power of
the divine love. All of them, however, spoke with a knowledge that came to them not through intellectual arguments
but through contemplative prayer. The Spirit of Jesus allowed them to see the heart of God, the heart of the universe, and their own hearts as one. It is in the heart of God
that we can come to the full realization of the unity of
all that is, created and uncreated.

Ministry and the Spiritual Life

All Jesus' words and actions emerge from his intimate relationship with his Father. "Do you not believe," Jesus says, "that I am in the Father and the Father is in me? What I say to you I do not speak of my own accord: it is the Father, living in me, who is doing his works. You must believe me when I say that I am in the Father and the Father is in me; or at least believe it on the evidence of these works" (John 14:10–11).

Just as all Jesus' words and actions emerge from his communion with his Father, so all our words and actions must emerge from our communion with Jesus. "In all truth I tell you," he says, "whoever believes in me will perform the same works as I do myself, and will perform even greater works. . . . Whatever you ask for in my name I will do" (John 14:12–13). It is this profound truth that reveals the relationship between the spiritual life and the life of ministry.

❦

Acting in the Name of Jesus

Ministry is acting in the Name of Jesus. When all our actions are in the Name, they will bear fruit for eternal life. To act in the Name of Jesus, however, doesn't mean to act as a representative of Jesus or as his spokesperson. It means to act in an intimate communion with him. The Name is like a house, a tent, a dwelling. To act in the Name of Jesus, therefore, means to act from the place where we are united with Jesus in love. To the question "Where are you?" we should be able to answer, "I am in the Name." Then, whatever we do cannot be other than ministry because it will always be Jesus himself who acts in and through us. The final question for all who minister is, "Are you in the Name of Jesus?" When we can say yes to that, all of our lives will be ministry.

❧

Active Waiting

Waiting is essential to the spiritual life. But waiting as a disciple of Jesus is not an empty waiting. It is a waiting with a promise in our hearts that makes already present what we are waiting for. We wait during Advent for the birth of Jesus. We wait after Easter for the coming of the Spirit, and after the ascension of Jesus we wait for his coming again in glory. We are always waiting, but it is a waiting in the conviction that we have already seen God's footsteps.

Waiting for God is an active, alert—yes, joyful—waiting. As we wait we remember him for whom we are waiting, and as we remember him we create a community ready to welcome him when he comes.

Waiting with Patience

How do we wait for God? We wait with patience. But patience does not mean passivity. Waiting patiently is not like waiting for the bus to come, the rain to stop, or the sun to rise. It is an active waiting in which we live the present moment to the full in order to find there the signs of the One we are waiting for.

The word *patience* comes from the Latin verb *patior,* which means "to suffer." Waiting patiently is suffering through the present moment, tasting it to the full, and letting the seeds that are sown in the ground on which we stand grow into strong plants. Waiting patiently always means paying attention to what is happening right before our eyes and seeing there the first rays of God's glorious coming.

Waiting in Expectation

Waiting patiently for God includes joyful expectation. Without expectation our waiting can get bogged down in the present. When we wait in expectation our whole beings are open to be surprised by joy.

All through the Gospels Jesus tells us to keep awake and stay alert. And Paul says, "Brothers and sisters . . . the moment is here for you to stop sleeping and wake up, because by now our salvation is nearer than when we first began to believe. The night is nearly over, daylight is on the way; so let us throw off everything that belongs to the darkness and equip ourselves for the light" (Romans 13:11–12). It is this joyful expectation of God's coming that offers vitality to our lives. The expectation of the fulfillment of God's promises to us is what allows us to pay full attention to the road on which we are walking.

The Challenge of Aging

Waiting patiently in expectation does not necessarily get easier as we become older. On the contrary, as we grow in age we are tempted to settle down in a routine way of living and say, "Well, I have seen it all. . . . There is nothing new under the sun. . . . I am just going to take it easy and live the days as they come." But in this way our lives lose their creative tension. We no longer expect something really new to happen. We become cynical or self-satisfied or simply bored.

The challenge of aging is waiting with an ever-greater patience and an ever-stronger expectation. It is living with an eager hope. It is trusting that through Christ "we have been admitted into God's favour . . . and look forward exultantly to God's glory" (Romans 5:2).

Waiting for Christ to Come

If we do not wait patiently in expectation for God's coming in glory, we start wandering around, going from one little sensation to another. Our lives get stuffed with newspaper items, television stories, and gossip. Then our minds lose the discipline of discerning between what leads us closer to God and what doesn't, and our hearts lose their spiritual sensitivity.

Without waiting for the second coming of Christ, we will stagnate and become tempted to indulge in whatever gives us a moment of pleasure. When Paul asks us to wake from sleep, he says, "Let us live decently, as in the light of day; with no orgies or drunkenness, no promiscuity or licentiousness, and no wrangling or jealousy. Let your armour be the Lord Jesus Christ, and stop worrying about how your disordered natural inclinations may be fulfilled" (Romans 13:13–14). When we have the Lord to look forward to, we can already experience him in the waiting.

Waiting to Be Lifted Up with Christ

Waiting for Christ's second coming and waiting for the resurrection are one and the same. The second coming is the coming of the risen Christ, raising our mortal bodies with him in the glory of God. Jesus' resurrection and ours are central to our faith. Our resurrection is as intimately related to the resurrection of Jesus as our belovedness is related to the belovedness of Jesus. Paul is very adamant on this point. He says, "If there is no resurrection of the dead, then Christ cannot have been raised either, and if Christ has not been raised, then our preaching is without substance, and so is your faith" (1 Corinthians 15:13–14).

Indeed, our waiting is for the risen Christ to lift us up with him in his eternal life with God. It is from the perspective of Jesus' resurrection and our own that his life and ours derive their full significance. "If our hope in Christ has been for this life only," Paul says, "we are of all people the most pitiable" (1 Corinthians 15:18). We don't need to be pitied, because as followers of Jesus we can look far beyond the limits of our short lives on earth and trust that nothing we are living now in the body will go to waste.

❧

The Hidden Resurrection

The resurrection of Jesus was a hidden event. Jesus didn't rise from the grave to baffle his opponents, to make a victory statement, or to prove to those who crucified him that he was right after all. Jesus rose as a sign to those who loved him and followed him that God's divine love is stronger than death. To the women and men who committed themselves to him, he revealed that his mission had been fulfilled. To those who shared in his ministry, he gave the sacred task to call all people into the new life with him.

The world didn't take notice. Only those whom he called by name, with whom he broke bread, and to whom he spoke words of peace were aware of what happened. Still, it was this hidden event that freed humanity from the shackles of death.

Wounds Becoming Signs
of Glory

The resurrection of Jesus is the basis of our faith in the resurrection of our bodies. Often we hear the suggestion that our bodies are the prisons of our souls and that the spiritual life is the way out of these prisons. But by our faith in the resurrection of the body we proclaim that the spiritual life and the life in the body cannot be separated. Our bodies, as Paul says, are temples of the Holy Spirit (see 1 Corinthians 6:19) and, therefore, sacred. The resurrection of the body means that what we have lived in the body will not go to waste but will be lifted up in our eternal life with God. As Christ bears the marks of his suffering in his risen body, our bodies in the resurrection will bear the marks of our suffering. Our wounds will become signs of glory in the resurrection.

❦

Having Reverence and Respect for the Body

In so many ways we use and abuse our bodies. Jesus' coming to us in the body and his being lifted with his body into the glory of God call us to treat our bodies and the bodies of others with great reverence and respect.

God, through Jesus, has made our bodies sacred places where God has chosen to dwell. Our faith in the resurrection of the body, therefore, calls us to care for our own and one another's bodies with love. When we bind one another's wounds and work for the healing of one another's bodies, we witness to the sacredness of the human body, which is destined for eternal life.

Our Mortal Bodies, Seeds for the Resurrection

Our mortal bodies, flesh and bones, will return to the earth. As the writer of Ecclesiastes says, "Everything goes to the same place, everything comes from the dust, everything returns to the dust" (Ecclesiastes 3:20). Still, all that we have lived in our bodies will be honored in the resurrection, when we receive new bodies from God.

What sorts of bodies will we have in the resurrection? Paul sees our mortal bodies as the seeds for our resurrected bodies: "What you sow must die before it is given new life; and what you sow is not the body that is to be, but only a bare grain, of wheat I dare say, or some other kind; it is God who gives it the sort of body that he has chosen for it, and for each kind of seed its own kind of body" (1 Corinthians 15:36–38). We will be as unique in the resurrection as we are in our mortal bodies, because God, who loves each of us in our individuality, will give us bodies in which our unique relationship with God will gloriously shine.

Our Lives, Sowing Times

Our short lives on earth are sowing times. If there were no resurrection of the dead, everything we live on earth would come to nothing. How can we believe in a God who loves us unconditionally if all the joys and pains of our lives are in vain, vanishing in the earth with our mortal flesh and bones? Because God loves us unconditionally, from eternity to eternity, God cannot allow our bodies— the same as that in which Jesus, his Son and our savior, appeared to us—to be lost in final destruction.

No, life on earth is the time when the seeds of the risen body are planted. Paul says, "What is sown is perishable, but what is raised is imperishable; what is sown is contemptible but what is raised is glorious; what is sown is weak, but what is raised is powerful; what is sown is a natural body, and what is raised is a spiritual body" (1 Corinthians 15:42–44). This wonderful knowledge that nothing we live in our bodies is lived in vain holds a call for us to live every moment as a seed of eternity.

Spiritual Bodies

In the resurrection we will have spiritual bodies. Our natural bodies came from Adam, our spiritual bodies come from Christ. Christ is the second Adam, offering us new bodies not subject to destruction. As Paul says, "As we have borne the likeness of the earthly man [Adam], so we shall bear the likeness of the heavenly one [Christ]" (1 Corinthians 15:49).

Our spiritual bodies are Christ-like bodies. Jesus came to share with us the life in our mortal bodies so that we would also be able to share in his spiritual body. "Mere human nature," Paul says, "cannot inherit the kingdom of God" (1 Corinthians 15:50). Jesus came to dress our perishable nature with imperishability and our mortal nature with immortality (see 1 Corinthians 15:53). Thus, it is in the body that our spiritual life finds its fullest manifestation.

DECEMBER

❧

Meeting the Risen Christ

When Jesus appeared to his disciples after his resurrection, he convinced them that he was not a ghost but the same one that they had known as their teacher and friend. To his frightened and doubtful friends he said, "See by my hands and my feet that it is I myself. Touch me and see for yourselves" (Luke 24:39). Then he asked them for something to eat, and later, when he appeared to them for the third time, he offered them breakfast, bread and fish (see Luke 24:42–43 and John 21:12–14).

But Jesus also showed them that his body was a new spiritual body, no longer subject to the laws of nature. While the doors of the room where the disciples had gathered were closed, Jesus came and stood among them (see John 20:19), and when he offered them breakfast, nobody dared to ask, "Who are you?" They knew it was Jesus, their Lord and teacher, but they also knew that he no longer belonged to their world (see John 21:12). It was this experience of the risen Jesus that revealed to his disciples the life in the resurrection that was awaiting them. Are there any experiences in our lives that give us a hint of the new life that has been promised us?

❦

The Dilemma of Life

Do we desire to be with Christ in the resurrection? It seems that most of us are not waiting for this new life but instead are doing everything possible to prolong our mortal lives. Still, as we grow more deeply into the spiritual life—the life in communion with our risen Lord—we gradually get in touch with our desire to move through the gate of death into eternal life with Christ. This is no death wish but a desire for the fulfillment of all desires. Paul strongly experienced that desire. He writes, "Life to me, of course, is Christ, but then death would be a positive gain. . . . I am caught in this dilemma: I want to be gone and to be with Christ, and this is by far the stronger desire—and yet for your sake to stay alive in this body is a more urgent need" (Philippians 1:21–24). This is a dilemma that few of us have, but it lays bare the core of the spiritual struggle.

Death, a New Birth

There comes a time in all our lives when we must prepare for death. When we become old, get seriously ill, or are in great danger, we can't be preoccupied simply with the question of how to get better unless "getting better" means moving on to a life beyond death. In our culture, which in so many ways is death oriented, we find little if any creative support for preparing ourselves for a good death. Most people presume that our only desire is to live longer on this earth. Still, dying, like giving birth, is a way to new life, and as Ecclesiastes says, "There is a season for everything: . . . a time for giving birth, a time for dying" (Ecclesiastes 3:1–2).

We have to prepare ourselves for our death with the same care and attention as our parents prepared themselves for our birth.

Nurturing the Eternal Life Within Us

The knowledge that Jesus came to dress our mortal bodies with immortality must help us develop an inner desire to be born to a new, eternal life with him and encourage us to find ways to prepare for it.

It is important to nurture constantly the life of the Spirit of Jesus—which is the eternal life—that is already in us. Baptism gave us this life, the Eucharist maintains it, and our many spiritual practices—such as prayer, meditation, spiritual reading, and spiritual guidance—can help us to deepen and solidify it. The sacramental life and life with the Word of God gradually make us ready to let go of our mortal bodies and receive the mantle of immortality. Thus, death is not the enemy who puts an end to everything but the friend who takes us by the hand and leads us into the Kingdom of eternal love.

❧

Giving Permission to Die

One of the greatest gifts we can offer our family and friends is helping them to die well. Sometimes *they* are ready to go to God but *we* have a hard time letting them go. But there is a moment in which we need to give those we love the permission to return to God, from whom they came. We have to sit quietly with them and say, "Do not be afraid . . . I love you, God loves you . . . it's time for you to go in peace. . . . I won't cling to you any longer . . . I set you free to go home. . . . Go gently, go with my love." Saying this from the heart is a true gift. It is the greatest gift love can give.

When Jesus died he said, "Father, into your hands I commit my Spirit" (Luke 23:46). It is good to repeat these words often with our dying friends. With these words on their lips or in their hearts, they can make the passage as Jesus did.

God's Timeless Time

There is no "after" after death. Words like *after* and *before* belong to our mortal life, our life in time and space. Death frees us from the boundaries of chronology and brings us into God's "time," which is timeless. Speculations about the afterlife, therefore, are little more than that: speculations. Beyond death there is no "first" and "later," no "here" and "there," no "past," "present," or "future." God is all in all. The end of time, the resurrection of the body, and the glorious coming again of Jesus are no longer separated by time for those who are no longer in time.

For us who still live in time, it is important not to act as if the new life in Christ is something we can comprehend or explain. God's heart and mind are greater than ours. All that is asked of us is trust.

❦

Restored to Eternal Life

One thing we know for sure about our God: Our God is a God of the living, not of the dead. God is life. God is love. God is beauty. God is goodness. God is truth. God doesn't want us to die. God wants us to live. Our God, who loves us from eternity to eternity, wants to give us life for eternity.

When that life was interrupted by our unwillingness to give our full yes to God's love, God sent Jesus to be with us and to say that great yes in our name and thus restore us to eternal life. So let's not be afraid of death. There is no cruel boss, vengeful enemy, or cruel tyrant waiting to destroy us—only a loving, always forgiving God, eager to welcome us home.

The Renewal of the Whole Creation

Our final homecoming involves not just ourselves and our fellow human beings but all of creation. The full freedom of the children of God is to be shared by the whole earth, and our complete renewal in the resurrection includes the renewal of the universe. That is the great vision of God's redeeming work through Christ.

Paul sees the whole created order as a woman groaning in labor, waiting eagerly to give birth to a new life. He writes, "It was not for its own purposes that creation had frustration imposed on it, but for the purposes of him who imposed it—with the intention that the whole creation itself might be freed from its slavery to corruption and brought into the same glorious freedom as the children of God" (Romans 8:20–21). All that God has created will be lifted up into God's glory.

Being Sisters and Brothers of Nature

When we think of oceans and mountains, forests and deserts, trees, plants and animals, the sun, the moon, the stars, and all the galaxies as God's creation, waiting eagerly to be "brought into the same glorious freedom as the children of God" (Romans 8:21), we can only stand in awe of God's majesty and God's all-embracing plan of salvation. It is not just we, human beings, who wait for salvation in the midst of our suffering; all of creation groans and moans with us, longing to reach its full freedom.

In this way we are indeed brothers and sisters not only of all other men and women in the world but also of all that surrounds us. Yes, we have to love the fields full of wheat, the snowcapped mountains, the roaring seas, the wild and tame animals, the huge redwoods, and the little daisies. Everything in creation belongs, with us, to the large family of God.

❦

The Peaceable Kingdom

All of creation belongs together in the arms of its Creator. The final vision is that not only will all men and women recognize that they are brothers and sisters called to live in unity but all members of God's creation will come together in complete harmony. Jesus the Christ came to realize that vision. Long before he was born, the prophet Isaiah saw it:

> The wolf will live with the lamb,
> the panther lie down with the kid,
> calf, lion and fat-stock beast together,
> with a little boy to lead them.
> The cow and the bear will graze,
> their young will lie down together.
> The lion will eat hay like the ox.
> The infant will play over the den of the adder;
> the baby will put his hand into the viper's lair.
> No hurt, no harm will be done
> on all my holy mountain,
> for the country will be full of knowledge of Yahweh
> as the waters cover the sea.   (Isaiah 11:6–9)

We must keep this vision alive.

A New Heaven and a New Earth

Long before Jesus was born the prophet Isaiah had a vision of Christ's great unifying work of salvation. Many years after Jesus died, John, the beloved disciple, had another but similar vision: He saw a new heaven and a new earth. All of creation had been transformed, dressed with immortality to be the perfect bride of Christ. In John's vision the risen Christ speaks from his throne, saying, "Look, I am making the whole of creation new. . . . Look, here God lives among human beings. He will make his home among them; they will be his people, and he will be their God, God-with-them. He will wipe away all tears from their eyes; there will be no more death, and no more mourning or sadness or pain. The world of the past has gone" (Revelation 21:5; 21:3–4).

Both Isaiah and John open our eyes to the all-inclusive nature of Christ's saving work.

Energizing Visions

Are the great visions of the ultimate peace among all
people and the ultimate harmony of all creation just
utopian fairy tales? No, they are not! They correspond to
the deepest longings of the human heart and point to the
truth waiting to be revealed beyond all lies and deceptions.
These visions nurture our souls and strengthen our hearts.
They offer us hope when we are close to despair, courage
when we are tempted to give up on life, and trust when
suspicion seems the more logical attitude. Without these
visions our deepest aspirations, which give us the energy
to overcome great obstacles and painful setbacks, will be
dulled and our lives will become flat, boring, and finally
destructive. Our visions enable us to live the full life.

Anticipating the Vision

The marvelous vision of the peaceable Kingdom, in which all violence has been overcome and all men, women, and children live in loving unity with nature, calls for its realization in our day-to-day lives. Instead of being an escapist dream, it challenges us to anticipate what it promises. Every time we forgive our neighbor, every time we make a child smile, every time we show compassion to a suffering person, every time we arrange a bouquet of flowers, offer care to tame or wild animals, prevent pollution, create beauty in our homes and gardens, and work for peace and justice among peoples and nations we are making the vision come true.

We must remind one another constantly of the vision. Whenever it comes alive in us we will find new energy to live it out, right where we are. Instead of making us escape real life, this beautiful vision gets us involved.

Heaven and Hell

Is everybody finally going to be all right? Are all people ultimately going to be free from misery and all their needs fulfilled? Yes and no! Yes, because God wants to bring us home into God's Kingdom. No, because nothing happens without our choosing it. The realization of the Kingdom of God is God's work, but for God to make God's love fully visible in us, we must respond to God's love with our own love.

There are two kinds of death: a death leading us into God's Kingdom, and a death leading us into hell. John in his vision saw not only heaven but also hell. He says, "The legacy for cowards, for those who break their word, or worship obscenities, for murderers and the sexually immoral, and for sorcerers, worshippers of false gods or any other sort of liars, is the second death in the burning lake of sulphur" (Revelation 21:8). We must choose for God if we want to be with God.

❧

The Good News of Hell

Is there a hell? The concepts of heaven and hell are as intimately connected as those of good and evil. When we are free to do good, we are also free to do evil; when we can say yes to God's love, the possibility of saying no also exists. Consequently, when there is heaven there must also be hell.

All these distinctions are made to safeguard the mystery that God wants to be loved by us in freedom. In this sense, strange as it may sound, the idea of hell is good news. Human beings are not robots or automatons who have no choices and who, whatever they do in life, end up in God's Kingdom. No, God loves us so much that God wants to be loved by us in return. And love cannot be forced; it has to be freely given. Hell is the bitter fruit of a final no to God.

❧

The Freedom to Refuse Love

Often hell is portrayed as a place of punishment and heaven as a place of reward. But this concept easily leads us to think about God as either a policeman, who tries to catch us when we make a mistake and send us to prison when our mistakes become too big, or a Santa Claus, who counts up all our good deeds and puts rewards in our stockings at the end of the year.

God, however, is neither a policeman nor a Santa Claus. God does not send us to heaven or hell depending on how often we obey or disobey. God is love and only love. In God there is no hatred, desire for revenge, or pleasure in seeing us punished. God wants to forgive, heal, restore, show us endless mercy, and see us come home. But just as the father of the prodigal son let his son make his own decision, God gives us the freedom to refuse God's love, even at the risk of destroying ourselves. Hell is not God's choice. It is ours.

☙❦☙

A Second Death

Hell is a second death. This is what the Book of Revelation says (see Revelation 21:8). Just as there is an eternal life, there is an eternal death. Eternal life is a second life; eternal death is a second death. Our first death can be a passage not only to eternal life but also to eternal death.

Looking at hell as a second death takes away the images of eternal suffering and torture that are so prevalent in medieval art and literature. It defines hell more as the refusal to choose life than as a punishment for wrongdoing. In fact, the sins that the Book of Revelation mentions as leading to eternal death are choices for death: murdering, worshiping obscenities, sexual immorality, lying, and so on (see Revelation 21:8). When we sow death we will reap death. But when we sow life we will reap life. It is we who do the sowing!

The Fullness of Time

Jesus came in the fullness of time. He will come again in the fullness of time. Wherever Jesus, the Christ, is the time is brought to its fullness.

We often experience our time as empty. We hope that tomorrow, next week, next month, or next year the real things will happen. But sometimes we experience the fullness of time. That is when it seems that time stands still; that past, present, and future become one; that everything is present where we are; and that God, we, and all that is have come together in total unity. This is the experience of God's time. "When the completion of the time came [that is, in the fullness of time], God sent his Son, born of a woman" (Galatians 4:4), and in the fullness of time God will "bring everything together under Christ, as head, everything in the heavens and everything on earth" (Ephesians 1:10). It is in the fullness of time that we meet God.

The Mountaintop Experience

At some moments we experience complete unity within us and around us. This may happen when we stand on a mountaintop and are captivated by the view. It may happen when we witness the birth of a child or the death of a friend. It may happen when we have an intimate conversation or a family meal. It may happen in church during a service or in a quiet room during prayer. But whenever and however it happens we say to ourselves, "This is it . . . everything fits . . . all I ever hoped for is here."

This is the experience that Peter, James, and John had on the top of Mount Tabor when they saw the aspect of Jesus' face change and his clothing become sparkling white. They wanted that moment to last forever (see Luke 9:28–36). This is the experience of the fullness of time. These moments are given to us so that we can remember them when God seems far away and everything appears empty and useless. These experiences are true moments of grace.

❦

Seeing God for Others

The experience of the fullness of time, during which God is so present, so real, so tangibly near that we can hardly believe that everyone does not see God as we do, is given to us to deepen our lives of prayer and strengthen our lives of ministry. Having experienced God in the fullness of time, we have a lifelong desire to be with God and to proclaim to others the God we experienced.

Peter, years after the death of Jesus, claims his Mount Tabor experience as the source for his witness. He says, "When we told you about the power and the coming of our Lord Jesus Christ, we were not slavishly repeating cleverly invented myths; no, we had seen his majesty with our own eyes ... when we were with him on the holy mountain" (2 Peter 1:16–18). Seeing God in the most intimate moments of our lives is seeing God for others.

An Experience Offered to All

Some people say, "I never had an experience of the fullness of time. . . . I am just an ordinary person, not a mystic." Although some people have unique experiences of God's presence and, therefore, have unique missions to announce God's presence to the world, all of us—whether learned or uneducated, rich or poor, visible or hidden—can receive the grace of seeing God in the fullness of time. This mystical experience is not reserved for a few exceptional people. God wants to offer that gift in one way or another to all God's children.

But we must desire it. We must be attentive and interiorly alert. For some people the experience of the fullness of time comes in a spectacular way, as it did to St. Paul when he fell to the ground on his way to Damascus (see Acts 9:3–4). But for some of us it comes like a murmuring sound or a gentle breeze touching our backs (see 1 Kings 19:13). God loves us all and wants us all to know this in a most personal way.

Light in the Darkness

We walk in a "ravine as dark as death" (Psalm 23:4), and still we have nothing to fear because God is at our side: God's staff and crook are there to soothe us (see Psalm 23:4). This is not just a consoling idea. It is an experience of the heart that we can trust.

Our lives are full of suffering, pain, disillusions, losses and grief, but they are also marked by visions of the coming of the Son of Man "like lightning striking in the east and flashing far into the west" (Matthew 24:27). These moments in which we see clearly, hear loudly, and feel deeply that God is with us on the journey make us shine as a light into the darkness. Jesus says, "You are the light of the world. Your light must shine in people's sight, so that, seeing your good works, they may give praise to your Father in heaven" (Matthew 5:14–16).

The Heart of Jesus

Jesus is the vulnerable child, the humble preacher, the despised, rejected, and crucified Christ. But Jesus is also "the image of the unseen God, the first-born of all creation . . . [who] exists before all things and in him all things hold together" (Colossians 1:15, 17). Jesus is the King, ridiculed on the cross and reigning from his throne in the heavenly Jerusalem. He is the Lord riding into the city on a donkey, and the Alpha and Omega, the Beginning and the End. He is cursed by the world but blessed by God.

Let's always look at Jesus, because in his crucified and glorified heart we will see ourselves called to share in his suffering as well as in his glory.

❦

Holding On to the Christ

Life is unpredictable. We can be happy one day and sad the next, healthy one day and sick the next, rich one day and poor the next, alive one day and dead the next. So who is there to hold on to? Who is there to feel secure with? Who is there to trust at all times?

Only Jesus, the Christ. He is our Lord, our shepherd, our rock, our stronghold, our refuge, our brother, our guide, and our friend. He came from God to be with us. He died for us, he was raised from the dead to open for us the way to God, and he is seated at God's right hand to welcome us home. With Paul, we must be certain that "neither death nor life, nor angels, nor principalities, nothing already in existence and nothing still to come, nor any power, nor the heights nor the depths, nor any created thing whatever, will be able to come between us and the love of God, known to us in Christ Jesus our Lord" (Romans 8:38–39).

❧

The Task of Reconciliation

What is our task in this world as children of God and brothers and sisters of Jesus? Our task is reconciliation. Wherever we go we see divisions among people—in families, communities, cities, countries, and continents. All these divisions are tragic reflections of our separation from God. The truth that all people belong together as members of one family under God is seldom visible. Our sacred task is to reveal that truth in the reality of everyday life.

Why is that our task? Because God sent Jesus to reconcile us with God and to give us the task of reconciling people with one another. As people reconciled with God through Jesus we have been given the ministry of reconciliation (see 2 Corinthians 5:18). So whatever we do the main question is, "Does it lead to reconciliation among people?"

Claiming Our Reconciliation

How do we work for reconciliation? First and foremost by claiming for ourselves that God through Christ has reconciled us to God. It is not enough to believe this with our heads. We have to let the truth of this reconciliation permeate every part of our beings. As long as we are not fully and thoroughly convinced that we have been reconciled with God, that we are forgiven, that we have received new hearts, new spirits, new eyes to see, and new ears to hear, we continue to create divisions among people because we expect from them a healing power they do not possess.

Only when we fully trust that we belong to God and can find in our relationship with God all that we need for our minds, hearts, and souls can we be truly free in this world and be ministers of reconciliation. This is not easy; we readily fall back into self-doubt and self-rejection. We need to be constantly reminded through God's Word, the sacraments, and the love of our neighbors that we are indeed reconciled.

A Nonjudgmental Presence

To the degree that we accept that through Christ we ourselves have been reconciled with God we can be messengers of reconciliation for others. Essential to the work of reconciliation is a nonjudgmental presence. We are not sent to the world to judge, to condemn, to evaluate, to classify, or to label. When we walk around as if we have to make up our minds about people and tell them what is wrong with them and how they should change, we only create more division. Jesus says it clearly, "Be compassionate just as your Father is compassionate. Do not judge; . . . do not condemn; . . . forgive" (Luke 6:36–37).

In a world that constantly asks us to make up our minds about other people, a nonjudgmental presence seems nearly impossible. But it is one of the most beautiful fruits of a deep spiritual life and will be easily recognized by those who long for reconciliation.

Being Safe Places for Others

When we are free from the need to judge or condemn, we can become safe places for people to meet in vulnerability and take down the walls that separate them. Being deeply rooted in the love of God, we cannot help but invite people to love one another. When people realize that we have no hidden agendas or unspoken intentions, that we are not trying to gain any profit for ourselves, and that our only desire is for peace and reconciliation, they may then find the inner freedom and courage to leave their guns at the door and enter into conversation with their enemies.

Many times this happens even without our planning. Our ministry of reconciliation most often takes place when we ourselves are least aware of it. Our simple, nonjudgmental presence does it.

A Ministry That Never Ends

Reconciliation is much more than a one-time event by which a conflict is resolved and peace established. A ministry of reconciliation goes far beyond problem solving, mediation, and peace agreements. There is not a moment in our lives without the need for reconciliation. When we dare to look at the myriad hostile feelings and thoughts in our hearts and minds, we will immediately recognize the many little and big wars in which we take part. Our enemy can be a parent, a child, a "friendly" neighbor, people with different lifestyles, people who do not think as we think, speak as we speak, or act as we act. They all can become "them." Right there is where reconciliation is needed.

Reconciliation touches the most hidden parts of our souls. God gave reconciliation to us as a ministry that never ends.

Letting Go of Old Hurts

One of the hardest things to do in life is to let go of old hurts. We often say, or at least think, "What you did to me and my family, my ancestors, or my friends I cannot forget or forgive. . . . One day you will have to pay for it." Sometimes our memories are decades, even centuries, old and keep asking for revenge.

Holding people's faults against them often creates an impenetrable wall. But listen to Paul: "For anyone who is in Christ, there is a new creation: the old order is gone and a new being is there to see. It is all God's work" (2 Corinthians 5:17–18). Indeed, we cannot let go of old hurts, but God can. Paul says, "God was in Christ reconciling the world to himself, not holding anyone's faults against them" (2 Corinthians 5:19). It is God's work, but we are God's ministers, because the God who reconciled the world to God entrusted to us "the message of reconciliation" (2 Corinthians 5:19). This message calls us to let go of old hurts in the Name of God. This is the message our world most needs to hear.

God's Imagination

So much of our energy, time, and money goes into maintaining distance from one another. Many if not most of the resources of the world are used to defend ourselves against one another, to maintain or increase our power, and to safeguard our own privileged position.

Imagine all that effort being put in the service of peace and reconciliation! Would there be any poverty? Would there be crimes and wars? Just imagine that there was no longer fear among people, no longer rivalry, hostility, bitterness, or revenge. Just imagine all the people on this planet holding hands and forming one large circle of love. We say, "I can't imagine." But God says, "That's what I imagine, a whole world not only created but also living in my image."

A Final Prayer

"In the abundance of his glory may God, through his Spirit, enable us to grow firm in power with regard to our inner selves, so that Christ may live in our hearts through faith, and then, planted in love and built on love, with all God's holy people we will have the strength to grasp the breadth and the length, the height and the depth; so that, knowing the love of Christ, which is beyond knowledge, we may be filled with the utter fullness of God. Glory be to him whose power, working in us, can do infinitely more than we can ask or imagine; glory be to him from generation to generation in the Church and in Christ Jesus for ever and ever. Amen" (Ephesians 3:16–21).

❦